UNDERGROUND FIRE

HOPE, SACRIFICE, AND COURAGE IN THE CHERRY MINE DISASTER

SALLY M. WALKER

CANDLEWICK PRESS

IN HONOR OF THE MANY THOUSANDS OF IMMIGRANTS—
PAST, PRESENT, AND FUTURE—
FOR THEIR CONTRIBUTIONS THAT MAKE THE UNITED STATES
A VIBRANT AND RICHLY DIVERSE NATION

AND IN MEMORY OF MY GREAT-GRANDFATHER
DAVID MACART, WHO WAS A HOISTING ENGINEER
IN A PENNSYLVANIA COAL MINE

Text copyright © 2022 by Sally M. Walker
Map and diagram illustrations (pp. iv, 18–19, 41, 48, 51, and 55)
copyright © 2022 by Rita Csizmadia

Image credits appear on page 215.

First edition 2022

Library of Congress Catalog Card Number 2021953461
ISBN 978-1-5362-1240-2

22 23 24 25 26 27 LEO 10 9 8 7 6 5 4 3 2 1

Printed in Heshan, Guangdong, China

This book was typeset in Century Old Style.

Candlewick Press
99 Dover Street
Somerville, Massachusetts 02144

www.candlewick.com

A JUNIOR LIBRARY GUILD SELECTION

CONTENTS

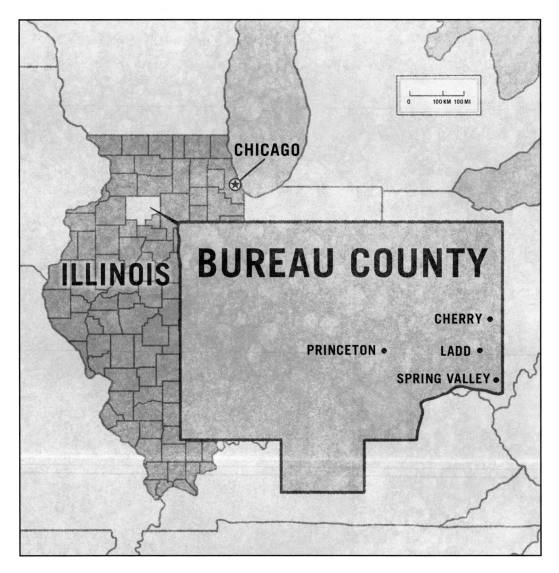

Mining towns such as Cherry, Ladd, and Spring Valley, in the southeast corner of Bureau County, Illinois, bustled with activity in the early twentieth century. Their mines provided coal for homes, factories, and railroads.

CHAPTER 1

SATURDAY, NOVEMBER 13, 1909

Shortly before dawn on Saturday, November 13, 1909, many people in Cherry, Illinois, were already out of bed, despite chilly air and a cloudy sky. Soon, the day shift would start at Cherry Mine.

Celina Howard served breakfast to her sons, Sam and Alfred. Twenty-year-old Sam had worked in the mine for several years.

Fifteen-year-old Alfred had recently started work there as a trapper, a person who opens certain trapdoors in a mine. He should not have been hired: sixteen was the youngest that a boy could legally work in a coal mine. But his mother had requested a special certificate from Alfred's teacher. Celina had signed the certificate, which stated that Alfred was sixteen years old, and given it to the mine manager. Celina Howard wasn't the only parent who had signed a similar certificate so

Sam Howard

an underage son could work in the mine. Food, housing, and clothing for a family often cost more than what one wage earner (at that time, usually a man) could make. Even though John Bundy, the mine manager, suspected—even knew—that Alfred was underage, he took the certificate and hired Alfred. Since Celina's divorce, Alfred's daily wage of $1.13 was much-needed additional income for the family of seven.

Celina packed her sons' metal lunch pails with bread, a slice or two of meat or cheese, perhaps a piece of pie or cake, and a container of water. As the brothers left home, Sam may have glanced down the street, toward the home of his girlfriend, Mamie Robinson. He and Mamie were planning a Christmas wedding. Sam was going to give her an engagement ring in the next few days.

Miners carried their food and a container of water inside a metal lunch pail.

A few blocks away, on Steele Street, Jessie Love said goodbye to her husband, John, and his three brothers, and to her brothers, Robert and Alexander Deans. Like most of the miners' homes, the Loves' house—one of thirty-three identical houses that lined one side of Steele Street—had five rooms. Downstairs there was a small kitchen, a parlor, and a room many families used as an extra bedroom. Upstairs, two bedrooms crowded under the roof. Jessie and John Love, their two children, plus the couple's five brothers filled the house to the brim.

For many Cherry homeowners, a houseful of people was not unusual. To supplement miners' wages, some homeowners rented a room—or even just sleeping space—to relatives or to other miners. If a man dug a root cellar beneath his house, he could rent that space too! In exchange for a place to live, Robert and Alexander Deans gave

Although one side of Steele Street was lined with a row of identical houses, the majority of the miners' homes in Cherry were constructed in five different architectural styles.

Dunbar Photo
Princeton, Ill.

"Dead Row"
In this Row of 30 Cottages only 4 Men Survived
the Disaster Nov 13, 1909   Cherry Ill.

their wages to their sister to help with household expenses. That morning, the six men stepped off the Loves' front stoop and mingled with the throng already walking toward the mine on Cherry's packed-dirt streets.

Not far away, Antenore Quartaroli said "ciao" or "arrivederci"—Italian for "see you later"—to his wife, Erminia, and his infant son. Quartaroli had learned a lot of English in the seven years he'd lived in Illinois, but like most Italian immigrants,

Antenore Quartaroli

his family and friends spoke Italian among themselves.

When the coal company had planned the town of Cherry, it provided a number of company-owned houses that would be available to rent to miners who had a family. Some of the houses came from a coal-mining neighborhood in Centerville, Iowa. Carpenters cut them apart, loaded them onto railroad cars, and shipped them to Cherry, where they were reassembled. Company carpenters built more houses on-site, in Cherry. The company assigned the houses it owned to a miner and his family for ten dollars per month. Antenore Quartaroli rented his house from the company.

Alex Norberg

That morning, after Antenore left, Erminia probably went outside for water to wash the breakfast dishes. Every two company-owned houses shared a well, located in one of the backyards. None of the homes had indoor plumbing, so there was an outhouse in the back as well.

When Antenore left his house, he may have joined his next-door neighbor, Giacomo Pigati, and Giacomo's brother, Salvatore, who worked the day shift too. The Pigati brothers had emigrated from Italy almost ten years earlier. Giacomo was proud that he and his wife, also an Italian immigrant, owned their home in Cherry. Like most houses in town, the Pigatis' did not have electricity. The family lit their home with candles and kerosene lamps. Rosalie Pigati cooked on a coal-burning stove that also heated the house. Unlike the Quartarolis, the Pigatis (and other homeowners) had their own well.

Several blocks away, fourteen-year-old Albert Buckel and his older brother, Richard, were on their way to the mine. Like Celina Howard, Albert and Richard's mother, Mary, had signed special certificates for them, one a few years previously for Richard, and another recently for Albert. The boys' father, Otto, had been a blacksmith employed at the mine. Since his death several years earlier, the boys' wages were crucial for the family's survival.

Alex Norberg was on his way to the mine too. As an assistant mine manager, Norberg regularly checked with the miners under his supervision to make sure the work was running smoothly. When Norberg had started work-

Isaac "Ike" Lewis

ing at Cherry Mine, he commuted from a nearby town. But the year before, his family had moved to Cherry, renting the house next door to the one owned by his brother-in-law, Ike Lewis. Sisters Anna Norberg and Mary Lewis and their children often went back and forth between the houses. Although Ike no longer worked in the mine, he was probably awake. He owned a livery stable, and the horses needed to be fed early in the morning. Perhaps Ike and Alex walked up the street together.

Four doors down the same street, Ike's brother, Herbert, was probably getting ready to leave for work. Herbert had also left mining. But his job as a teamster required an early start. His horses delivered wagonloads of coal cinders to Cherry's homes and businesses. The cinders would be burned in the stoves that were used to heat the buildings.

Plenty of people were outside when a loud, shrill whistle pierced the air. The whistle signaled that Cherry Mine's hoisting cages were ready to lower day-shift workers into the mine. At the whistle's blast, men and boys already in the streets walked faster. Others hurried from their homes and boardinghouses. The last cage into the mine descended at 7:00 a.m. No one wanted to miss it.

Six years earlier, a crowd would not have been walking toward the mine. No mine existed then, and there was no Cherry, Illinois. In 1903, there was only a handful of farms clustered near a country crossroads. Cornstalks, scattered trees, and barns were the tallest things in sight. Farmers grew corn and raised cows, chickens, and pigs.

By 1905, the area near the crossroads had changed dramatically. Within months, the town of Cherry seemed to spring out of nowhere. Houses like the Love, Howard, and Quartaroli homes lined newly scraped dirt roads. Business lots along wide Main Street were selling like hotcakes. There was a general store that sold groceries and a selection of many other items. By the time Cherry was seven weeks old, its population had grown to six hundred. Town planners predicted Cherry would have one thousand to two thousand residents within two years.

Money in a New Town

CHERRY, ILLINOIS

ARE you looking for a real estate investment? Would you like to own a business or residence lot in a new town in Northern Illinois within 138 miles of Chicago, in the heart of one of the richest farming communities in Illinois—a town that is certain to be one of the principal coal mining centers of the Middle West within a year?

The town of Cherry, Ill., is located on the Rochelle & Southern Railway, which connects with the Chicago, Milwaukee & St. Paul Railway at Davis Junction, Ill.

The St. Paul Coal Company, which is owned and controlled by the Chicago, Milwaukee & St. Paul Railway, has completed sinking one of the largest coal mines in Illinois, at Cherry. This mine will have a capacity of upwards of 2,000 tons of coal every working day of eight hours the entire year. The tower is built of steel, foundation of concrete, and engine, boiler and fan houses of stone and brick, all absolutely fireproof. The construction and equipment, both on top and below, is of the most modern and up-to-date pattern. The St. Paul Coal Company has built fifty modern, model houses and a large modern hotel for the miners.

All the output of this mine will be used by the Chicago, Milwaukee & St. Paul Railway. This will give constant employment to between 600 and 700 men, summer and winter.

LOTS BY AUCTION, JUNE 21

I have 120 acres of land at Cherry for sale. This land will be divided into business lots of 25 by 130 feet and residence lots of 50 by 130 feet, with alleys 20 feet in width. The main business street will be 100 feet wide and the other streets 66 feet. The main business street will be graded, graveled and curbed, with concrete sidewalks on each side. Other streets will be graded and packed with steel roller.

Wednesday, June 21 (10:30 a. m.), is the date set for auction of these lots. If you are interested in the matter, it would be well to fill out the enclosed coupon and mail it to me at once for additional information.

It would be better to take a trip to Cherry and inspect the opening there before making any investment. It would be best for you to plan to be present at the auction and buy a piece of real estate that will advance in value from the date coal shipments are made.

Send coupons or address letters of inquiry for additional information to

J. W. BLEE
Sandwich, Illinois

Name_____

Street Address _____

Town_____ State_____

Business or residence lot desired _____

Amount of money to be invested_____

Trade to be represented_____

Newspapers throughout Illinois carried ads that encouraged people to move to the newly created town of Cherry.

By 1908, more houses had been built. More families moved in. More stores—selling groceries, meat, hardware, and clothing—opened, as did a post office, a barbershop, two churches, and a number of saloons. More than two hundred students in first through eighth grades filled the brick school's four classrooms.

By Saturday, November 13, 1909, Cherry's population had neared twenty-five hundred. The sleepy country crossroads owed its transformation into a lively, busy town to an exciting discovery: coal!

After just a few months, stores and saloons lined Cherry's Main Street. Cherry's planners promised that Main Street would eventually have a fairly unusual feature: cement sidewalks. The wooden poles that edge the sidewalk are for hitching horses.

CHAPTER 2
FROM CORNFIELDS TO COAL MINE

In 1903, word of mouth spread the news that coal—
a black or brown rock that can be burned as fuel—was buried
beneath the area that surrounded the country crossroads. Three
veins of coal, layered like the "lean streaks of meat in a strip of
bacon," lay hidden within the rock beneath the farmland. Coal ripe
for mining.

By then, coal was a vital part of most American lives. The population of the United States had soared from twenty-three million
people in 1850 to seventy-three million in 1900. In one way or another,
coal touched the lives of almost everyone in the country. Coal-
burning furnaces heated homes, apartments, hospitals, schools,
and other large buildings. Homemakers cooked meals on coal-
burning stoves. It fueled the engines of steam locomotives and

People who heated their homes and fueled their kitchen stoves with coal had it delivered on a regular basis. Coal stoves used for heating parlors and bedrooms were often placed within a fireplace.

the boilers of steamboats. The giant, steam-powered machinery in factories was also fueled with burning coal. People everywhere demanded coal. More and more coal mines opened. In 1860, US coal mines produced about 11.3 million tons of coal. By 1900, they produced 302.5 million tons a year, and that still wasn't enough.

The Chicago, Milwaukee, and St. Paul Railroad, one of the Midwest's biggest railroad companies, wanted a reliable source of coal for its locomotives. The company's officers decided to open a coal mine. They formed a new branch of the organization and named it the St. Paul Coal Company.

The St. Paul Coal Company bought hundreds of acres of farmland in Bureau County, Illinois, and made plans to construct buildings and two mine shafts near the country crossroads. The company also bought the mineral rights from the people who owned thousands of adjoining acres. Farmers and others still owned the surface of the land, but they sold the coal beneath to the St. Paul Coal Company. Buying these rights made it legal for the company to remove the coal. From the mine's shaft located on company land, miners could tunnel under adjoining land and dig out the coal.

Cherry Mine—named after James Cherry, the superintendent of the company—was three miles north of Ladd, an established coal-mining town. Ladd was the site of the Chicago, Milwaukee, and St. Paul Railroad's large regional rail yard. The railroad's busy main line ran past the town. Workers connected Cherry Mine to Ladd with a new set of tracks. Railroad cars on this line would carry Cherry Mine's coal to the main line, where it would be shipped elsewhere.

Trains from Cherry carried people and coal to nearby Ladd. Connections there carried both to other places.

Mine superintendent James Cherry hired John Bundy as the mine manager. Bundy was an experienced coal miner who had emigrated from Wales many years earlier. James Cherry had heard about Bundy's exemplary work in another Illinois mine, and he wanted a knowledgeable man for the manager's job at Cherry Mine.

Word that Cherry Mine was hiring spread quickly. In 1904, brothers Herbert and Ike Lewis, who at that time lived a few miles away, were among the first who joined the crew. Both had worked as miners.

Alex Norberg, who had emigrated from Sweden nearly fifteen years earlier, worked in the coal mine in nearby Spring Valley. Alex Norberg's wife and Ike Lewis's wife were sisters. Perhaps Norberg heard from Lewis that Cherry Mine was hiring. Norberg was hired as an assistant mine manager.

Everything about the new mine sounded good to men seeking work. The company planned a modern mine. Part of its tunnels would even be lit with electric light bulbs! The brick buildings on the surface were fireproof. Best of all, Cherry mine was going to provide year-round employment for up to seven hundred miners. Since there was less demand for coal during the summer months, other Illinois mines only offered work for about two hundred days a year. But all of Cherry Mine's coal was sold to the St. Paul Coal Company's parent company, the Chicago, Milwaukee, and St. Paul Railroad, which needed coal year-round. Employment at Cherry Mine meant a paycheck all year long.

SHAFTS AND TUNNELS

During the next five years, the work crew at Cherry Mine grew. A mine is more than just underground tunnels. Aboveground, carpenters and masons constructed buildings that were necessary to operate the mine. The brick boiler house provided the steam energy that operated the cages that carried workers into and up from the mine. The boilers also heated the buildings. When finished, the boiler house contained a line of boilers.

The fan house, located next to the air shaft, was equally important. A sixteen-foot state-of-the-art fan inside the building blew fresh air down the air shaft. The breeze it created was strong enough to blow out a match if a miner lit one while standing at the base of the air shaft. The windy current is a lifesaver. Coal veins contain methane gas. Methane forms as plant materials turn into coal. Miners call the gas "black damp." When black damp seeps from a coal vein, it fills the space that oxygen—fresh air—normally fills. People and animals that breathe black damp suffocate and die from lack of oxygen.

Even as work continued aboveground on buildings that included carpenter and blacksmith shops, an office, and a hospital, steam shovels scooped soil and loose rock, digging two deep holes about 225 feet apart. They were the mine's shafts. When the shafts became too deep for steam shovels, miners like the Lewis brothers, Antenore Quartaroli, and Giacomo Pigati gouged the rock with pickaxes and

The huge boilers in the mine's boiler house heated water, converting it into steam, which was used to power the mine's machinery. Six chimneys, used in rotation, belched clouds of exhaust, or leftover, steam high into the air outside.

steam-powered drills. Rock dust clouded the air and made the men spit grit.

The larger of the two shafts became the hoisting shaft and was the main entrance into the mine. Workers rimmed it with a five-foot-thick concrete collar to prevent it from caving in. Carpenters and metalworkers built a large raised building called the tipple above the hoisting shaft. The tipple contained the equipment that would lower men into the mine and lift them out, as well as the area where mined rock would be sorted and cleaned.

The wooden building on the right was the mine office. It's where miners received pay vouchers and money for their work. The boiler house chimneys and the tipple are behind the office. The semicircular fan house is on the left.

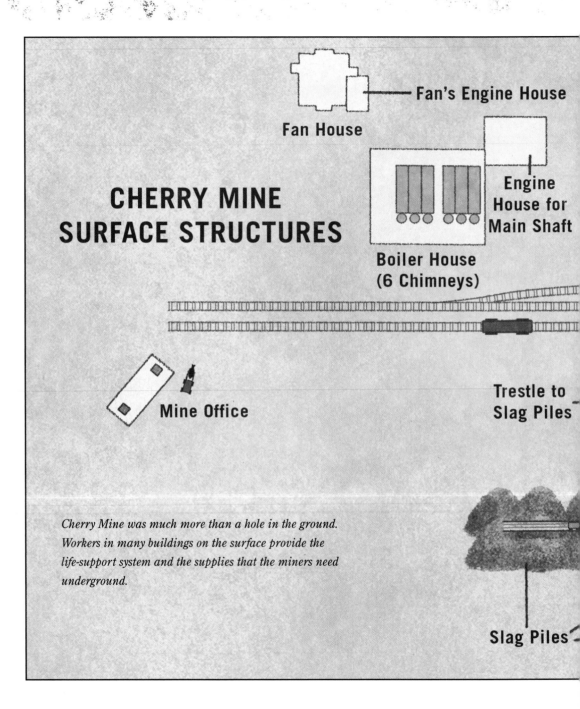

CHERRY MINE SURFACE STRUCTURES

Fan's Engine House

Fan House

Engine House for Main Shaft

Boiler House (6 Chimneys)

Trestle to Slag Piles

Mine Office

Slag Piles

Cherry Mine was much more than a hole in the ground. Workers in many buildings on the surface provide the life-support system and the supplies that the miners need underground.

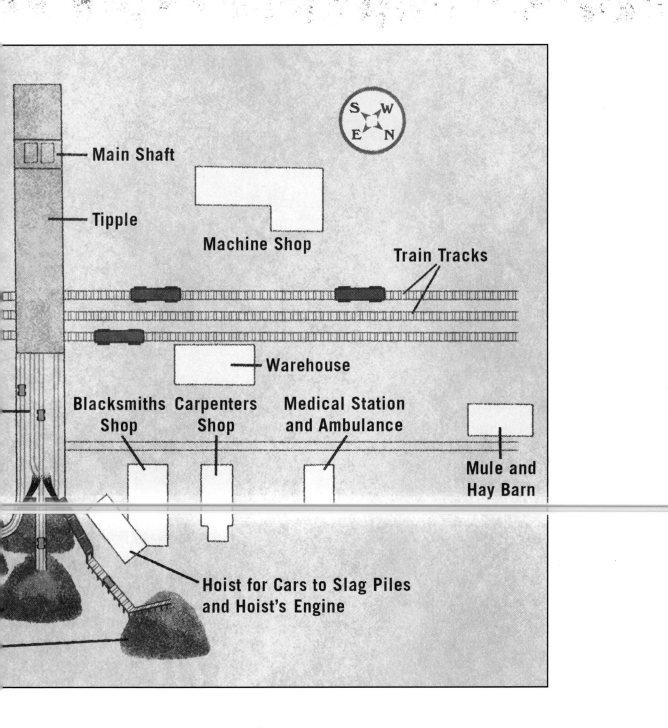

Main Shaft

Tipple

Machine Shop

Train Tracks

Warehouse

Blacksmiths Shop

Carpenters Shop

Medical Station and Ambulance

Mule and Hay Barn

Hoist for Cars to Slag Piles and Hoist's Engine

As the miners dug deeper, shaft carpenters nailed pine timbers into a framework that divided the hoisting shaft into two vertical compartments. They hung a wooden cage, attached to a steel cable, in each compartment. The long cable that connected the two cages was wrapped around a winding wheel high inside the tipple. When moving, the cages counterbalanced each other: one cage rose while the other descended. Miners entered and left the mine in these cages, which also lifted mined rock to the surface.

Cherry Mine had three veins of coal. The company decided not to mine the shallowest vein, since the coal was poor quality. A second vein, at 320 feet below the surface, was three to four feet thick and much better quality. Finally, 485 feet below the surface, the miners reached the third vein. At first, the St. Paul Coal Company planned to dig from that vein because it contained the best quality coal. But because the second vein contained a tremendous amount of coal, they decided to mine from the second vein right away.

Although the hoisting and air shafts extended down to the third vein, the framework inside the hoisting shaft did not go any lower than the second vein. This meant that the two cages could not go lower than the bottom of the second vein. The company planned to extend the framework needed for the cages when the third vein was fully opened.

The second shaft that the steam shovels and miners had dug was the air shaft. Half the size of the hoisting shaft, the air shaft was also divided into two vertical compartments. One compartment funneled fresh air—blown by the fan in the fan house—down into the mine. A single cage hung in this compartment. It did not go up to the surface;

The State of Illinois Bureau of Labor Statistics included this cross-sectional diagram of the mine in its report of the events that occurred on November 13, 1909. Although the coal veins in this diagram look completely horizontal, in some areas they slanted.

a Fan.   *b* Escape shaft.   *c* Third vein hoisting shaft and air shaft.   *d* Timbers closing first vein.   *e* Trap door at the top of the stairway on second level.   *f* Torch where hay caught fire. *g* Small cage to be attached to main cage above.   *h* Hook for attaching to main cage. *i* Sumps.   *j* Main hoisting shaft.

it only went up and down between the second and third veins. A steep wooden staircase filled the air shaft's other compartment. Besides the hoisting shaft, this staircase was the only other way to exit the mine.

During the next two years, miners like Giacomo and Salvatore Pigati carved an underground network of tunnels in the second vein that extended north, south, east, and west from the hoisting shaft. John Bundy and Alex Norberg organized and supervised the mining crews while they monitored the progress of other crews laying iron railroad tracks along the tunnels' floors.

George Eddy

At night, George Eddy took charge as mine examiner and fire boss. Born in England, Eddy immigrated to the United States as a young teen. By the time he was hired at Cherry Mine, he had more than twenty years of mining experience. Eddy's job was mine safety. Throughout the night, he checked the mine's condition. He tested for traces of toxic gas. He inspected timbers, noting any that needed replacement. He examined tunnel ceilings for signs of crumbling rock.

For coal miners, danger was a fact of life. Sections of crumbly shale ceilings collapsed. If a miner was lucky, he escaped a cave-in with a broken arm or leg. Wooden pit cars slipped and rolled. They crushed fingers, hands, and feet. John Bundy knew mine hazards firsthand. Before coming to Cherry, he'd broken a shoulder in an underground accident.

Families dreaded news of cave-ins, fires, and other tunnel disasters. In August 1905, Cherry Mine had its first tragedy. One man was severely injured at his work area; he later died in the hospital. Although shaken, his fellow miners returned to work the next day. They had no choice: mining coal provided food and shelter for their families.

On December 11, 1905, Cherry Mine was officially open and producing coal. By the end of 1907, the St. Paul Coal Company employed more than five hundred workers. That year, miners removed 348,951 tons of coal from Cherry Mine, more than any other mine in northern Illinois. Their record haul beat the previous year's winner by 351 tons. Cherry Mine had become a star thanks to its industrious employees!

From 1905 to 1909, Cherry Mine and the town of Cherry dramatically changed. The *Chicago Daily Tribune* had predicted, "Within a few years Cherry will be the greatest coal mining town in the central west." Its prediction came true. More and more people hired on at the mine and moved to town. Herbert and Ike Lewis and Alex Norberg, as well as other miners who already lived in the area, were familiar faces. But many of those who came were strangers. And that made some longtime Illinoisans uneasy. Who were these new people? Where had they come from?

Workers usually entered and left the mine in the hoisting shaft's cage.

FOREIGNERS

By the last half of the nineteenth century, people around the world regarded the United States as a land of hope and opportunity, a place where people could own land and find employment. In some countries, a large number of men were unemployed. Families became so poverty-stricken that one meal a day, if that, was all they could afford. People who lived in these conditions were willing to risk everything to find a better life in America.

At first, most of the immigrants who arrived on the United States' East Coast came from Germany, Scotland, England, Wales, Ireland, and Scandinavia. Some, such as Albert and Richard Buckel's father, Otto, came unmarried, without a family. He emigrated from Germany in 1881 and quickly found work as a blacksmith in Nebraska. Several years later, he married Mary, their mother, who was also a German immigrant. While Albert and Richard were both born in America, it's likely that German was the first language they spoke. About 1905, Cherry Mine's manager hired Otto as one of the company blacksmiths.

In contrast, John Love was already married when he immigrated in 1906. Like many immigrants, John came because a good friend who had emigrated from Scotland months earlier urged him to come. An experienced coal miner, John immigrated specifically to work in Cherry Mine. The mine's managers welcomed him because coal miners from Great Britain were trained to do several different jobs within a mine. John's wife, Jessie, and their two children immigrated

Gigantic steamships, fueled by coal, carried thousands of immigrants across the Atlantic Ocean. Accommodations in steerage, where passengers with the cheapest tickets stayed, were cramped and lacked privacy.

six months after John did. The Loves sent letters to their brothers in Scotland, urging them to immigrate too. Within three years, Jessie's two brothers and John's three brothers had immigrated to Cherry. John's brothers mailed their wages to their wives and children, who still lived in Scotland. Each brother's family planned to immigrate as soon as they had enough money to buy steamboat tickets to America and train tickets to Illinois.

The Loves and other immigrants who came from the United Kingdom and Ireland settled in fairly easily. They spoke English

Many immigrant families could not come to America together. The men would come first to work and earn enough money to pay the fares for their families to cross later.

as their native language. Most of them worshipped in Protestant churches, as did the majority of Americans at that time.

By the early 1900s, a steadily growing stream of new immigrants arrived. Some Americans worried that too many foreigners were coming. They worried that the foreigners would take their jobs. And they worried about who the new immigrants were. They came from unfamiliar European countries and seemed very different.

On May 29, 1903, the editorial page of the *Bureau County Tribune*, published in Princeton, Illinois—less than twenty miles from Cherry Mine—included a piece about immigration:

> *Never before in the history of this country was such a flood of immigration pouring into it as at the present time. . . . During the first seventeen days of May over 550,000 immigrants passed Ellis Island [New York], and the indications are that the total for the year will exceed 860,000 by the first day of June. . . . [T]he majority of it is . . . the most ignorant poverty stricken and superstitious [people] of Europe.*

People were leery of the new immigrants. They didn't speak English. Most were Roman Catholic, a Christian religion led by the pope. Roman Catholic worship services differed from Protestant services. How, people wondered, would these people fit in in America?

Eighty percent of the men hired to work at Cherry Mine were either born outside the United States or the sons of people who had been. Most came from Italy, Lithuania, England, Austria, Belgium, and Poland. As the Loves, Howards, Buckels, and Pigatis walked to the mine, they were as likely to hear people speaking Italian, German, French, Lithuanian, and Polish as they were to hear people speaking English.

While some Americans fretted about immigrants, coal companies welcomed them, even though most of them had little or no mining experience. Immigrants seldom complained about long hours or poor working conditions: they were happy to have a job. But a number of American miners resented them for those reasons, especially for their lack of experience. Coal mines are dangerous places; inexperience often leads to accidents.

Antenore Quartaroli, the Pigati brothers, and their wives were the kind of "foreigners" some people feared. While Quartaroli and the Pigati brothers had not been miners in Italy, they learned how to mine coal. They learned enough English to be understood.

On Saturday morning, November 13, 1909, when the mine's whistle blew, all of Cherry Mine's day-shift employees got dressed, ate breakfast, and went to work. Regardless of where they had been born or what language they spoke, they all shared the same goal: to earn wages that could be used to provide food and shelter for themselves and their families.

CHAPTER 3

INTO THE MINE

All the miners walking to work that Saturday morning saw the tipple. It was impossible to miss. Perched on stilts above the hoisting shaft, the long building had a ninety-foot tower that loomed above it. The tower contained the winding-wheel machinery that would lower Albert and Richard Buckel, Antenore Quartaroli, the Loves, and brothers Sam and Alfred Howard into the mine. As the men got closer, they also saw large piles of slag just beyond the tipple. Slag is unwanted rock material that does not contain coal.

Quartaroli, the Pigatis, the Loves, and the Howards had all contributed to the slag piles. Even though they had worked hard digging out the slag, coal companies only paid miners for coal. Belowground, miners put all the rock material they removed into large rolling containers called pit cars. Each miner had an identification tag that he attached to his pit car. When a pit car came up from the mine, workers in the tipple separated the coal from the slag. Then they washed the coal.

A man employed by the United Mine Workers—a national union that protected miners' rights—weighed each miner's coal and jotted the amount in a logbook. This man made sure that a miner was not shorted when his coal was weighed. A miner's wage depended on how much coal he mined. A pit car held about 1½ to 2 tons of rock.

Mules pulled pit cars deep in the mine. Like miners, they were lowered into the mine in the hoisting shaft's cages. Mules remained underground for weeks and months before returning to the surface. When not working, they stayed in stables located in the second and third veins. Hay was brought down to them daily. About seventy mules lived in Cherry Mine.

On a good day, two experienced miners could fill five carloads. After the slag was removed in the tipple, between 2,600 and 2,800 pounds of coal remained. The miners received $1.08 per ton of coal. Their total pay for eight hours of work would be about $3.50 each. They were paid twice monthly.

The washed coal was dumped into a railroad car placed below the tipple; a locomotive hauled it to Ladd. By that November morning, Cherry Mine was producing almost 1,500 tons of coal per day.

Just like these men, working in a mine in southern Illinois, men working in Cherry Mine's tipple separated coal from slag. After the coal was cleaned, it was dropped into railroad cars for shipment to Ladd.

Pit cars loaded only with slag rolled out of the tipple on an elevated track. At the track's end, a worker tipped the car and slag tumbled onto the pyramid-like slag piles. One pile was nearly fifty feet high. A separate track lay on that hill's steep side to haul slag to the top of the enormous pile. Many coal mine slag piles were left in place— rocky reminders of past underground activity. As years passed, those deemed landslide hazards were usually removed.

Overlooked pieces of coal ended up in slag heaps. Like these children in Pennsylvania, Cherry's children often climbed the piles, hunting for coal. Some were paid for the coal they collected; others brought it home to be used in their family's stove.

Albert and Richard Buckel joined the men waiting outside the hoisting shaft to board a cage and descend into the mine. A cager, the man responsible for loading and unloading a cage, counted them as they filed into the six-by-sixteen-foot cage. The hoisting shaft's other cage would have been down in the second vein. Two cagers were assigned to each cage: one at the top of the shaft, the other at the bottom, in the second vein. The cager counted until sixteen men—a full load—had boarded the cage. He then rang a signal bell a certain number of rings. This let the hoisting engineer in the engine house know he should lower the cage. A protective gate lowered and the cage slowly descended 320 feet to the second vein. As the Buckels traveled down, the cage in the other compartment rose to the surface, to be loaded with sixteen more men. The alternating cages carried all the day-shift workers to the second vein. It took about half an hour to get the entire shift down. That morning, 484 men descended into the mine.

The Buckel brothers weren't cold when they reached the second vein. While the air temperature on the surface was in the forties, the rock's temperature beneath the surface increased about one degree for every sixty feet of depth. In the second vein, Albert and Richard would have only needed a lightweight jacket, which they likely removed if they worked hard enough to sweat.

Deep in the mine, clammy air surrounded the brothers. Sandstone and shale, the rock that often surrounds coal veins, have tiny pores and cracks. Water seeps into these spaces, trickling down a mine's walls and puddling on the floor. In fact, coal mines have specially dug holes, called sumps, to catch this water so it can be pumped out of the mine. Without sumps and pumps, a coal mine would eventually flood.

Normally, the brothers had no trouble seeing when they reached the second vein. Unlike most Illinois coal mines at that time, Cherry Mine had electricity. In the second vein, light bulbs lit the main tunnel, or roadway, near the hoisting shaft, the mule stable, and the passageway between the hoisting and air shafts. Light bulbs also lit the air shaft from the second vein down to the third, which had been opened for digging coal in 1908. But several weeks earlier, water had penetrated the electric wire in Cherry Mine and shorted the system. New wire was on order but hadn't yet arrived. In the meantime, sixteen-inch pipe-like torches lit previously electrified areas. Wire attached to mine timbers held the torches horizontally in place. The torch's body was filled with a fuel called kerosene. A cotton wick, soaked by the kerosene, extended out from one end of the torch. When the wick was lit, a several-inch-long flame burned brightly. Mine manager John Bundy assigned cagers the task of placing and monitoring the torches. No one was particularly concerned about using torches; similar torches were routinely used in mines that did not have electricity.

Albert Buckel worked close to the hoisting shaft. He was the trapper for passageway doors about 250 feet east of the hoisting shaft. At certain places within a coal mine, ventilation doors are placed across passageways. These trapdoors are important because they control the direction of airflow in a mine. As a trapper, Albert's job was to open the doors for the mule drivers as they brought pit cars to and

As miners left Cherry's hoisting shaft, they walked along tunnels whose walls and ceilings were shored up with strong timbers. They passed pit cars along the way too.

from the miners to the hoisting shaft. A team of two or three mules pulled a train of pit cars along the iron tracks that lined floor of the passageways. When Albert reached his assigned doors, he said goodbye to Richard, who headed north into the passageway where he worked as a spragger.

Miners follow a coal vein as they dig. A vein can slant up or down within the rock that encases it. As a result, the floors of some passage-ways are slanted too. In tunnels with slanted floors, Richard ran alongside the pit cars. When a pit car stopped, he chocked its wheels with a short, pointed wooden stick, called a sprag, to prevent the

Like this young man in a West Virginia mine, Albert Buckel sat near a pair of trapdoors and listened for a mule driver's shout. For most of their hours-long shifts, trappers were in total darkness.

pit car from rolling away. Spragging was dangerous work. If Richard didn't time it just right, he could lose a finger—spraggers often did. Sometimes a miner asked a spragger to wedge a sprag into place as an additional ceiling support. Richard may have wedged sprags into the ceiling for Sam Howard, who also worked in the eastern portion of the second vein. Sam's brother, Alfred, was a trapper not far from the area where Sam worked.

Meanwhile, Antenore Quartaroli and his buddy, or mining partner, Francesco Zanarini, also left the cage and headed to their room, or workstation, in the second vein. Like most miners, they worked as a pair: one chiseled chunks of rock and coal with a pickax while the other loaded them into a pit car. By November 13, the grid of roadways and even narrower passageways in the second vein extended as far as three-quarters of a mile from the hoisting shaft. It could take a miner twenty minutes to reach his room. Quartaroli and Zanarini set out on that long walk.

Before Quartaroli and Zanarini reached their room, each lit the wick of a small lamp about three inches tall. The lamps were hooked to a bracket on the front of their caps. Earlier, each had filled his lamp with a fuel that miners called "sunshine." Sunshine is made of paraffin, the same waxy substance used to make candles. To fill his lamp, Quartaroli shaved pieces from the hard paraffin block and pushed them inside the lamp. Sunshine kept the lamp's wick burning for two to three hours before it needed a refill.

Before the buddies entered their room, they checked the flames of their lamps. A dim flame meant the level of oxygen in the room was

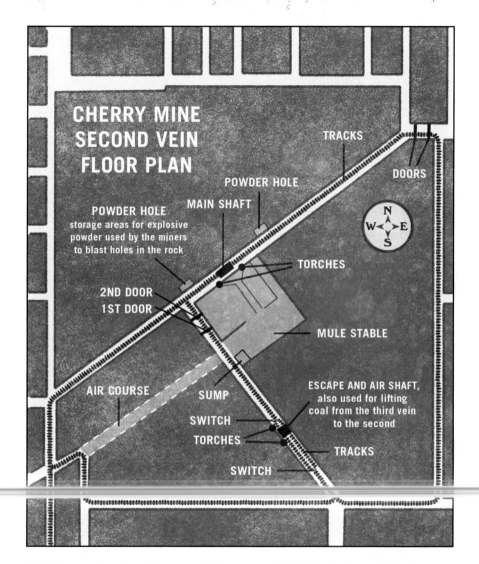

CHERRY MINE SECOND VEIN FLOOR PLAN

TRACKS

DOORS

POWDER HOLE

MAIN SHAFT

POWDER HOLE
storage areas for explosive
powder used by the miners
to blast holes in the rock

TORCHES

2ND DOOR
1ST DOOR

MULE STABLE

AIR COURSE

SUMP

ESCAPE AND AIR SHAFT,
also used for lifting
coal from the third vein
to the second

SWITCH

TORCHES

TRACKS

SWITCH

This diagram is adapted from one in the report published by the State of Illinois Bureau of Labor Statistics. It depicts the floor plan of the second vein, as if you were looking down on the vein. Mules hauled pit cars north, south, east, and west along underground tunnels. The entryways to the tunnels that led to the miners' workrooms can be seen along the perimeter of the diagram. Some of the tunnels were nearly a mile long.

low. A bright-blue flame meant the room contained methane gas—black damp. In either case, they wouldn't enter the room until the air was safe. That Saturday morning, the flame was a normal yellow. The buddies started work.

Quartaroli and the other miners who worked in the second vein removed coal in a way that created a series of underground rooms. They left twelve-foot-wide areas of unexcavated coal between the rooms. The unexcavated sections acted as pillars that supported the rock above and kept it from caving in. Since pillars were not mined, a lot of coal was left in the ground.

Before he began work, Antenore Quartaroli would stuff sunshine into a small lamp like this one. With a match, he would light the wick that he had tucked into the spout. He would then hook the burning lamp onto the front of his cap.

As Quartaroli and Zanarini chipped out rock, they supported the room's ceiling with timber planks. In most rooms, a miner couldn't stand, since the ceiling would not have been higher than the thickness of the coal vein.

Mule driver Charlie Thorne worked in the second vein too. That morning, he left the cage and went to the second vein's mule stable. (There was a stable in the third vein too.) He hitched his mules to a three-car train of empty pit cars. The mules hauled the cars along

A mule driver in a Pennsylvania mine leads his team through the ventilation doors. In Cherry Mine, when mule driver Charlie Thorne reached Albert Buckel's doors, he would holler for Buckel to open them. Depending on how many pit cars were being pulled, Thorne would hitch one, two, or three mules to the train.

another passageway to the air shaft, then back to the hoisting shaft. A round trip—empty cars to the air shaft, unhitching his mules and then hitching them to loaded cars, and returning to the hoisting shaft with the full cars—took Thorne about eight minutes.

Sometimes when Thorne was at the air shaft switching his teams, he chatted with Jessie Love's brother Robert Deans, who was the assistant cager at the air shaft. Deans helped roll empty pit cars into the cage that went down to the third vein, and rolled them off the cage when it returned with a full load. Several times that morning, Thorne exchanged how-do-you-dos with Albert Buckel when Albert opened the trapdoors for him.

Walter Waite

Assistant mine manager Walter Waite and his brother, Charlie, also left the cage at the second vein to begin work. They had emigrated from England almost twenty years earlier. Walter was among the most experienced miners at Cherry Mine. He was a highly respected pit boss. Charlie was a mine examiner and watched for safety issues. That morning, Walter headed off toward coal rooms in the southern part of the mine. He wanted to touch base with the miners and make sure work was proceeding smoothly. Charlie left to check another area of the second vein.

The cager at the top of the hoisting shaft later said a few more than three hundred men were working in the second vein.

The rest of the day-shift men who descended in the hoisting shaft cages that morning had to go even deeper, down to the third vein.

FOUR HUNDRED EIGHTY-FIVE FEET DOWN

After John Love, his three brothers, and the other assistant mine manager, Alex Norberg, reached the second vein, they left the hoisting shaft, walked past the mule stable, and continued on to the air shaft, more than 250 feet away. At the air shaft, they boarded a smaller cage. When the cage was full, cager Alexander Rosenjack signaled up to the air-shaft engineer to lower the cage to the third vein. That morning, Rosenjack lowered 181 men, in small groups, to the third vein. John Donna and his son, Peter, were among them.

John Donna and his wife had emigrated from Italy years before Peter's birth. Like Walter Waite, John had many years of experience in other Illinois coal mines. But foreigners who weren't from England or Scotland were seldom promoted to management jobs. When Donna hired on at Cherry Mine in 1909, sixteen-year-old Peter joined him as his buddy. Since the third vein had only been mined for about a year, the underground walk to their station took no more than six minutes.

Cherry Mine's mule stables probably looked similar to these two. Stall walls were often painted white to reflect the light and make the area appear brighter. Cherry Mine's electric lights were probably strung along the ceiling in a manner similar to those in these images.

The Donnas, Loves, and other miners in the third vein removed coal in a different pattern from the one used by miners in the second vein. Instead of creating rooms and pillars (which left coal behind), they worked along a long wall where the coal vein was continuously exposed. Miners working in adjacent areas progressed toward each other, chopping out the coal. When they eventually met, all the coal from that area of the vein had been removed.

Saturday morning, John used his pick to undercut a two-foot section of rock from beneath the coal vein. Without support, chunks of coal dropped to the floor when John chopped it.

Before John chiseled farther into the vein, he tapped the ceiling rock with his pick. If the tap sounded hollow, John supported the rock with an upright timber prop. Peter pushed a wood wedge into the gap between the prop and the ceiling to firmly hold the timber in place. The props remained there permanently and kept the Donnas safe from cave-ins.

While John picked, Peter shoveled the loose rock into the pit car left near their work area. He had attached their identification marker to the car. After Peter filled the morning's first car, a mule team hauled it to the cage in the air shaft, the only place where coal could be raised from the third vein. The company still hadn't extended the hoisting shaft framework all the way down to the third vein. A tiny, hard-to-connect emergency cage had been placed at the bottom of the hoisting shaft in the third vein a few weeks earlier. In an emergency, it could be lifted by connecting it to the bottom of one of the hoisting shaft's cages. But most of the miners didn't know it existed.

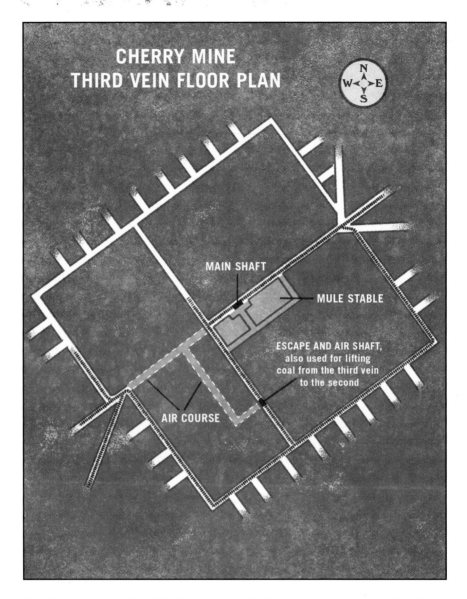

This diagram of a portion of the third vein, adapted from one in the report published by the State of Illinois Bureau of Labor Statistics, shows the air and escape shaft, which was the only way out of the third vein known to most of the miners who were working in that level. The tunnel entries along the perimeter of the diagram led to the miners' work areas.

When the Donnas' car was full, a mule train hauled it to the air shaft, and the third-vein cager rolled it into the cage. He signaled the engineer to raise it to the second vein, where cager Rosenjack or his helper Robert Deans rolled it off the cage.

Sixteen-year-old Matt Francesco worked as a coupler alongside Robert Deans. His job was attaching, or coupling, full cars into a train for Charlie Thorne. Francesco, like Albert Buckel and Alfred Howard, had started working in the mine as a trapper two years before, when he was fourteen. He'd just recently started work as a coupler at the air shaft. With three cars coupled together, Thorne's team of mules pulled the train with the Donnas' carload along the passageway to the hoisting shaft.

On Saturday morning at precisely 11:00, the mine whistle shrilled.

Time to eat lunch.

Like these miners in southern Illinois, Cherry's miners did not go to the surface during their lunch breaks. They brought their metal lunch pails into the mine with them.

At precisely 11:30, the whistle blew again.

Time to resume work.

Up in the tipple, a man carried bales of hay to the hoisting shaft. Every day at about 12:30 p.m., he sent down hay for the mules stabled in the third vein. Six bales of hay, standing on end, fit perfectly in a pit car. About half of each bale stuck up above the car's sides.

When the car of hay reached the second vein, Charlie Thorne hitched his team to it and headed along the track to the air shaft.

There were two sets of tracks at the air shaft. One set ran straight, across the opening where the third vein's cage was raised and lowered. The other tracks ran around the air shaft. An iron trapdoor, located between the rails of the runaround tracks, opened upward from the third vein. The staircase beneath the trapdoor was the way miners climbed down to and up from the third vein.

Just before Thorne reached the air shaft, he steered the team onto the runaround tracks and stopped. He unhitched the team from the hay car and left it on the runaround tracks, as he usually did. He knew Francesco or Deans would push it into the cage so cager Alexander Rosenjack could lower it to the third vein.

Thorne hitched his mules to a waiting train of loaded pit cars from the third vein. As the mules walked past the car containing the bales of hay, one of the mules stretched out its neck and snatched a bite. Thorne called out to the mules and they continued their trip back to the hoisting shaft.

Meanwhile, Francesco and Deans pushed the hay car farther along the runaround tracks. Usually they would have pushed the hay

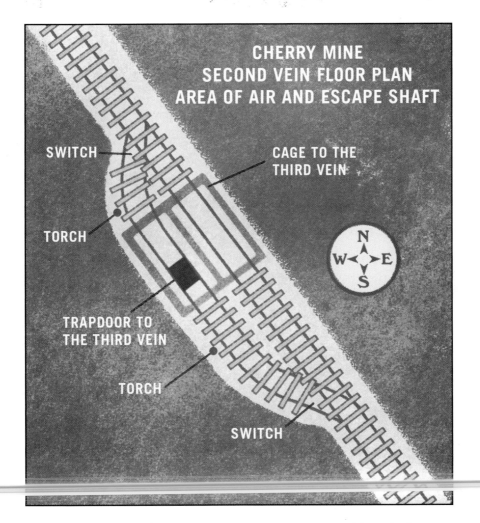

This diagram shows the air and escape shaft in the second vein, which provided access between the second and third veins. Two sets of tracks allowed the miners to maneuver the pit cars. One track was a runaround track that separated from and then reconnected to the main track. A trapdoor that raised upward was set flat between the rails of this track. Miners entered and left the third vein through the trapdoor. The pit car filled with bales of hay was on this track. Charlie Thorne parked the pit car loaded with hay bales near the torch. Then he unhitched his mules and hitched them to a car waiting inside the cage. That car was filled with coal that had just been brought up from the third vein.

car right into the cage. But the cage had just been raised and there was a full car on it. Before they could put the car containing the hay in the cage, Francesco and Deans had to push the coal-filled car off. They went to do that. The pit car filled with hay stood, unattended, either beside or directly below one of the kerosene torches.

As a rule, miners weren't particularly concerned that hay bales would catch fire. The hay bales sent into coal mines were very tightly compressed. So tightly that the hay resisted catching fire. So fire-resistant that the walls of some coal mine stables were built with bales of hay. Besides, the two young men didn't intend to leave the hay car there for very long.

Earlier, Francesco had seen kerosene dripping from the torch. That often happened when a torch was running low on fuel. When a torch's kerosene supply dwindled, someone—in this case Deans or Rosenjack, since John Bundy had assigned that job to the cagers—tipped the burning end of the torch toward the floor. That kept the supply of kerosene flowing down toward the wick. It wasn't uncommon to see a torch drip.

That morning, the dripping torch didn't worry Francesco, Deans, or Rosenjack.

It should have.

CHAPTER 4

TROUBLE

IN THE SECOND VEIN

Kerosene continued dripping. Within an hour, it had soaked the top of several hay bales. The steady stream of air flowing down the air shaft fanned the torch's flame, which lengthened and licked the hay. It began smoldering.

The trapdoor covering the staircase that led to the third vein opened. Finished for the day, several miners climbed a wooden ladder, a number of stairs, and finally a six-foot ladder that extended from the top of the staircase up to the trapdoor. They climbed out of the shaft and walked past the smoldering hay. They didn't pay much attention to it. Small mine fires were not uncommon; most of them were quickly extinguished. They didn't want to miss the 1:30 hoisting shaft cage; the next cage didn't go up until 3:30. They thought Alexander Rosenjack or Robert Deans would douse the fire.

By the time a few more third-vein miners emerged, Rosenjack, Deans, and Francesco had noticed the fire. Rosenjack asked one of the miners to help him move the smoldering car so men walking to the hoisting shaft could more easily pass it.

Meanwhile, flowing air blown down from the surface pushed smoke along the passages that led to the mule stable and hoisting shaft. Third-vein miners hurrying toward the hoisting shaft could scarcely see the way.

Back near the air shaft, Rosenjack and Deans pushed the hay car, by then in flame, toward the second vein sump hole. The sump was near the mule stable, about seventy-five feet away. Rosenjack planned to extinguish the fire with water from the sump. But the car's brass fittings were burning hot, too hot to touch.

Even worse, the flowing air had spread flames to the nearby timbers that supported the tunnel walls and ceiling.

Yelling "Fire! Fire!" Matt Francesco ran toward the stable, where he grabbed an empty lunch pail and filled it at the water trough in the stable.

Driver Charlie Thorne, on his return trip to the air shaft, saw the fire. He abandoned his mules and ran along his route to warn Albert Buckel. The two encountered Buckel's boss as they ran toward the hoisting cage.

"Bring your pail and we will run for water," his boss ordered.

"We tried to get in the barn for water, and there was too much smoke. We tried to get to the sump for water," Buckel later recalled.

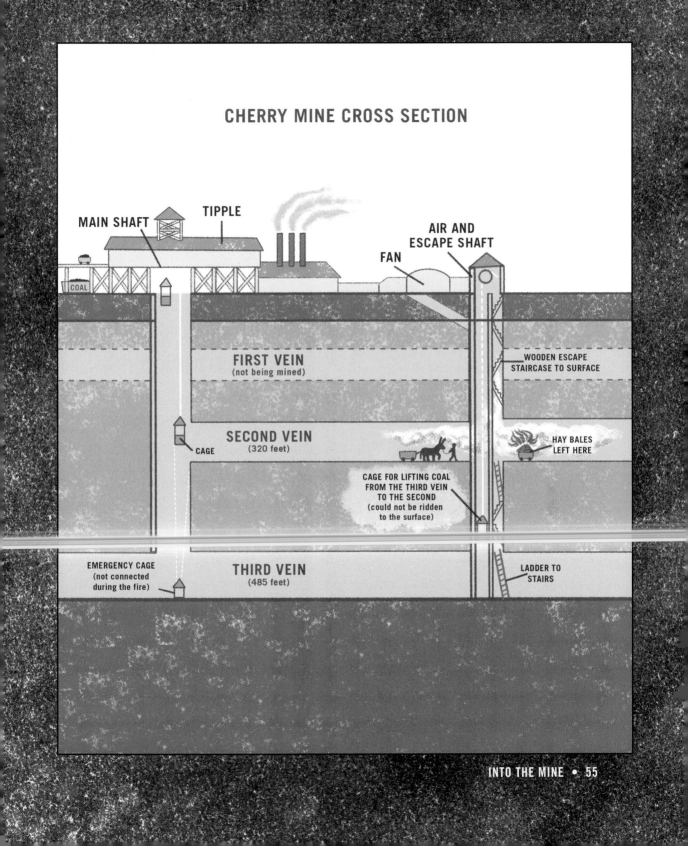

CHERRY MINE CROSS SECTION

MAIN SHAFT

TIPPLE

AIR AND
ESCAPE SHAFT

FAN

COAL

FIRST VEIN
(not being mined)

WOODEN ESCAPE
STAIRCASE TO SURFACE

CAGE

SECOND VEIN
(320 feet)

HAY BALES
LEFT HERE

CAGE FOR LIFTING COAL
FROM THE THIRD VEIN
TO THE SECOND
(could not be ridden
to the surface)

EMERGENCY CAGE
(not connected
during the fire)

THIRD VEIN
(485 feet)

LADDER TO
STAIRS

But the air current blew the fire's heat straight at them. They couldn't get close to the burning car.

Mine manager John Bundy was in the second vein. At first, he was unaware of the fire. As soon as he realized what was happening, he ordered Albert Buckel and others to go up. Buckel saw Bundy run toward the rooms in the west section of the mine to sound the alert. But some of the men there were working nearly a mile away. Would they have enough time to get out?

Meanwhile, two men had gone up to the surface and returned with a canvas hose. Unfortunately thick smoke and heat stopped them from reaching the stable. They tried to connect the hose to a nearby water pipe, but the end of the hose didn't fit the pipe. And they couldn't hold it in place because the pipe was burning hot.

Charlie Thorne and Albert Buckel had given up trying to carry water and stood at the hoisting cage.

"You'd better [h]eave us up," Thorne told one of the cagers.

"No, they may get the fire out and start to work again," the cager replied. For about ten minutes, the two cagers continued to send coal-filled cars up to the tipple.

One of the men waiting with Buckel turned away and started for the passageway where Albert's brother, Richard, and many others were working.

"I am going in there to tell the boys to tell the diggers to come out," he called back.

Back at the burning hay car, Matt Francesco had run as fast as he could, but his trip to the stable and back with a water-filled pail had taken more than five minutes. He threw the water onto the burning hay. But it didn't help.

Realizing buckets of water weren't going to work, cager Alexander Rosenjack decided the best way to handle the burning car was to send it down to the third vein. The water-filled sump hole for that vein was directly below, at the bottom of the air shaft. He went down in the air-shaft cage to the third vein to tell the cager there what he planned, leaving Robert Deans and Matt Francesco behind.

When the air-shaft cage came up again, one of the second-vein mule drivers struggled to push the burning car into it. Suddenly, miners climbing up from the third vein opened the trapdoor. The hay blazed from the sudden influx of more air. Swirling flames from both sides of the car reached toward the driver. It was so hot that he couldn't hang on. He grabbed a timber prop and used it to pull the car. He managed to get the car halfway into the cage. At that moment, he saw Robert Deans stagger and groan. Desperately in need of fresh air himself, the driver grabbed hold of Deans and headed for the hoisting shaft. The car kept burning as the two men staggered away.

DOWN IN THE THIRD VEIN

Down in the third vein, the cager and his assistant were still unaware of the fire 160 feet above. Men whose shift had ended stood around joking as they waited to leave. They were surprised when Alexander Rosenjack appeared.

"[We have] a car of hay up there afire," Rosenjack said. He told the cager his plan.

"Let it fall down," the cager replied. He said that his men would spray more water into the sump and put out the fire.

They sent the cage up and waited a few minutes, but nothing happened. By then, assistant mine manager Alex Norberg, who was working in the third vein, had joined them. Norberg shouted up the shaft but heard no answer. Concerned, he climbed the staircase to find out what was going on. Rosenjack and the others followed him up to the second vein to see if they could help.

UP IN THE SECOND VEIN

By that time, the cager at the hoisting shaft was worried. The heat was intense and smoke had flooded the main roadway to the hoisting shaft. Already, he had sent up a cage that contained, among others, Albert Buckel, Matt Francesco, and Charlie Thorne.

But something besides smoke worried the cager. Almost every day, coal miners drilled one or more small holes in the rock in their workstation. The men did this to prepare the rock for controlled blasts called shots. Later, they would pack the holes with a powder that explodes when it is exposed to fire. The force of the shots would fracture the rock, making it easier to chop with a pickax. For safety reasons, the miners often fired their shots just before their work shift ended. If the rock broke apart and fell, it would likely do so after the miners had left the area. The two storage areas for the mine's daily supply of explosive powder were located near the hoisting shaft. If the fire ignited the powder, it would explode. The cager and his assistant collected the explosive materials and loaded them into the cage.

Before the cager could signal the hoisting engineer at the top to raise the cage, Alex Norberg shouted for him to wait. Norberg had an urgent message. Send word up to the fan house. Tell the men there to slow the fan. Its strong current was spreading the fire. Norberg believed that slowing the fan could stop the fire's spread.

Back at the air shaft, Rosenjack opened the trapdoor to the second vein. He saw the burning hay car was halfway into the cage. Terrifyingly, the cage was on fire too!

Quickly, Rosenjack rang a signal of four bells to the engineer at the top of the air shaft. It meant "raise the cage slowly." As the cage rose higher, the burning car tipped more and more. Finally, in a shower of sparks, it slipped off the cage and plunged down the air shaft.

When Rosenjack and the others had first climbed through the trapdoor opening, they hadn't felt any air current. Norberg's request had been heeded. Would the fire stop spreading?

The men waited for the cagers in the third vein to call up to them that they'd successfully doused the burning hay-filled car.

DOWN IN THE THIRD VEIN

Minutes before, the cagers in the third vein had heard Rosenjack's signal bells, followed by a loud shout.

"Look out!"

A fire-fall of hay and burning timbers tumbled down the shaft and splashed into the sump. Smoke billowed around the men nearby. Coughing and struggling to breathe, one of the cagers grabbed the hose that was used to dampen coal dust on the passageway's floor and extinguished the fire.

When the men were sure the fire was completely out, one of them climbed up to the second vein to check conditions there. As soon as he cracked open the trapdoor, he noticed that the steady air current he usually felt when he lifted the door had stopped. Even worse, timbers blazed all along the hundred-foot passageway between the air shaft and the second-vein sump hole.

He dropped the door closed and went back to the third vein to warn the men working below.

At the bottom, he told the assistant cager that "the whole air course in the shaft [above] was all afire" and "it was best to get these men out as quickly as they could."

He ran along a tunnel until he saw the lights on miners' caps. He hollered, "Fire!" He yelled that everyone should get out. After sounding the alert, he hurried back to the escape staircase in the air shaft.

Meanwhile, in a different area in the third vein, John Donna had just gathered some ceiling props to hammer in place. But Peter smelled smoke and went out to the main passageway. Pieces of a heavy material called canvas hung across some of the passages. Similar to the way the trapdoors worked, the canvas was used to channel the flow of fresh air toward rooms where miners were working.

Peter pushed through hanging canvas and found thick smoke. He met the cager, who told him about the burned hay and the fire in the second vein.

Peter ran back to his father and told him they had to get out. John fussed and said he wanted to finish setting the props. Peter grabbed the tools and shoved them into their toolbox. John kept the box's key tied to his vest so it wouldn't get lost. Peter cut the key from his father's vest, locked the box, and strode toward the escape stairs. John, still irritated, followed.

The Donnas and others clustered around the bottom of the air shaft.

"I am getting no signals from above. Better go up the air-shaft stairs," the cager told them. The Donnas and the others started climbing. The cager remained behind.

"I won't go until every man is out of this mine," he told them. The four Love brothers and dozens of other men were still back in the tunnels.

UP IN THE SECOND VEIN

Peter and John Donna finally reached the top of the escape ladder and the second vein. It hadn't been easy. After the man climbing above Peter went through the iron trapdoor, he had dropped it on Peter. It knocked him down eight rungs. Fortunately, he didn't lose consciousness. He and John continued their climb. Before they even cleared the escape ladder, they realized that a direct run to the hoisting shaft was impossible. Flames engulfed the whole passageway.

They couldn't use the air shaft's narrow staircase from the second vein to the top either: the steps were completely on fire. Their only hope was to follow the route that Charlie Thorne normally took when he drove his team away from the air shaft. It was a long runaround roadway, but at least it led to the hoisting shaft.

The father and son's trip soon became a nightmare. The fan that Norberg had ordered turned off had been turned back on. Flowing air blew out the flames of the Donnas' sunshine lamps and they couldn't get them relit. Smoke obscured what little light the flickering fire behind them offered. Two panicked mules, still hitched to pit cars, had been abandoned in the roadway. They twisted and turned, trying to run away. Even if they had run, there was nowhere for them to go. As it was, they blocked the roadway. Men trying to escape were afraid to squeeze past them.

Luckily, a mule driver was with Peter and John. He shouldered the two mules aside. Peter grabbed a piece of timber and prodded them farther out of the way so more men could get through.

There was no light that far along the roadway, so Peter put his foot on one of the pit cars. Keeping contact with the rail, the Donnas followed the track to the main roadway that led to the hoisting shaft.

When they finally reached the main passageway, they had to climb over coal-filled cars and a five-mule team that had collapsed from smoke inhalation. Flames in the roadway singed their hair and eyebrows. They barely saw a sliver of light at the hoisting shaft cage. When he reached the hoisting cage, Peter didn't wait for a cager's permission. He and everyone with him tumbled into the cage, coughing and faint from lack of oxygen.

At the surface, Peter was horrified when he turned to help his father from the cage. John wasn't there! In the confusion at the bottom of the shaft, Peter hadn't realized that his father had stumbled and fallen. Peter tried to go back down, but men held him back. Relief swept through him when John stepped off the next cage up.

By then, it was about 2:00 p.m.

Half an hour earlier, Antenore Quartaroli and his buddy, Francesco Zanarini, still had no idea there was a problem. After a mule driver unhitched an empty car and left it for the buddies, Quartaroli had picked up his shovel and returned to work.

In an area far to the east, also in the second vein, Sam Howard had chipped coal. Nearby, his brother, Alfred, sat by his designated door and waited to open it for the next mule train through. The day seemed normal to them too.

In yet another area, far to the south, two buddies, John Lorimer and Thomas White, were also having what appeared to be a normal workday.

At that time, none of them knew that their lives were in danger. That smoke filled the roadway between the air shaft and the mule stable and surrounded the hoisting shaft. They had no idea that 50 to 60 of the 181 men working in the third vein had fled the mine. Or that the rest of the miners in the third vein were trapped below—with no way out.

CHAPTER 5

MEANWHILE, CONFUSION

Shortly before 1:30 p.m., the cager at the top of the hoisting shaft saw smoke drifting from the shaft. Then miners who got off the 1:30 cage said there was a fire near the air shaft. The cager quickly passed Alex Norberg's message—"stop the fan"—to the fan house.

Mine examiner George Eddy sat smoking his pipe about seventy-five feet from the hoisting shaft. He was off duty and had just finished his lunch. When Eddy saw the smoke, he took the next cage down to offer his help. Charlie Waite, also a mine examiner, had just come up from the second vein. He knew about the fire but returned with Eddy to find his brother, Walter, who he heard was still in the second vein.

Near the fan house, teamster Herbert Lewis began shoveling cinders into his wagon. He noticed that the mine's fan was stopped.

"What's the trouble here?" he asked.

"[There's a] car of hay on fire down below," a man answered. No one seemed particularly excited, so Lewis resumed shoveling.

As Norberg had ordered, the engineer had stopped the fan. But it had not stopped the fire's spread for long. Men told the engineer that flames had heated the passageways near the air and hoisting shafts to an unbearable level.

Robert Deans reached the surface and staggered away from the cage at about 1:45 p.m. Distraught, and still trying to catch his breath, Deans sobbed, "They are all lost down there." He feared for his brother-in-law John Love and John's three brothers, who were in the third vein.

When the hoisting shaft cagers in the second vein had first learned of the fire, they thought the pit bosses would quickly extinguish it. Believing this true, for a short time they'd continued sending coal-filled pit cars to the surface. Since then, both cages in the hoisting shaft were bringing men to the surface every five minutes. Even as men hurried from the cages, rumors spread throughout the crowd growing around the two shafts that coal was still being lifted.

"Hoist the men, not the coal!" people yelled. Company men roped off the main shaft to hold back the angry, worried crowd of townspeople who had arrived at the mine.

A fire drill had never been conducted at Cherry Mine, so there was mass confusion below as men fled the fire. Those who escaped told how they stumbled and crawled, feeling their way in the darkness because their lamps wouldn't stay lit. They described flames jumping from one ceiling timber to the next. Yet despite worsening conditions in the mine, some men who had escaped only remained on the surface long enough to catch their breath. Then they went back down to help others.

Meanwhile, in the second vein, Alexander Rosenjack, John Bundy, and Alex Norberg moved to the passageways that led toward the hoisting shaft. They heard people calling for help in German, Lithuanian, French, Italian, Polish, and English. They shouted to them, hoping the sound of their voices would draw the desperate men toward them. Those who reached them were overcome by smoke and too weak to walk any farther. Bundy and Norberg supported them to the cages.

By then, thick smoke filled the air; oxygen-starved men lay dying in the passageways. Alex Norberg realized that stopping the fan had not worked. He decided to try a new strategy. He ordered the fan reversed. Instead of blowing fresh air *down* into the mine, he hoped it would pull smoky air *up* and *out* of the mine. If this strategy worked, it might clear enough smoke from the roadways to enable men to find their way to the cages in the hosting shaft or the escape staircase in the air shaft.

Over the course of about an hour, almost 215 men escaped. Then a tragic consequence occurred. The reversed fan had pulled smoke away from the hoisting shaft and into the air shaft. But it also pulled in flames. Timbers in the air shaft caught fire and eventually turned the shaft into an inferno. The fan's metal blades heated to the point where the fan-house engineer feared parts weakened by the heat would break and send the spinning blades into the nearby crowd of people. The engineer had no choice. He stopped the fan.

After that, the hoisting shaft was the only way out of the mine.

Meanwhile, Rosenjack, Norberg, and Bundy rode up from the second vein for a short break. Without some fresh air, they wouldn't be able to continue their rescue work. Sweat-smeared coal dust streaked their faces. Fire had scorched their clothes. Rosenjack collapsed. He tried to stand, to get in the next cage down, but men held him back. He lay on the ground, crying and groaning. Some thought he wept because he regretted not paying closer attention to the position of the torch and the hay bales. Others thought it was because he wasn't permitted to go back down.

A group of men surrounded Norberg.

"The men are burning to death or dying by the gas and smoke! For God's sake do something for the poor devils and do it quick!" said Norberg. He said rescuers couldn't find men in the dark; they needed light.

Ike Lewis, Herbert's brother, had run over from his livery stable.

"Do you have a team [of horses] here?" he asked Herbert.

"Yes," answered Herbert.

"Go to my barn and get four or five lanterns, they need some lanterns down below."

While Herbert Lewis hurried to the livery, people surrounded the hoisting shaft. Mary Buckel saw people running toward the mine and heard them yelling about fire. She raced to the mine and

As news about the fire spread, a crowd of worried people from nearby houses and businesses hurried to the mine.

Mine Disaster Nov. 13, 1909

Dunham Photo
Princeton, Ill.

searched the growing crowd for her boys. She finally found Albert. He told her someone had run to warn Richard, but they couldn't find him among the crowd.

Frantic with worry, Celina Howard sought Sam and Alfred among the escaped miners. Sam's fiancée, Mamie Robinson, helped her search, but neither woman found them. Impatiently, they waited for the next cage to rise.

Mine examiner Charlie Waite's wife, Anna, was on her way out of the dentist's office. As she walked down the street, she saw her sister-in-law, Alma Norberg, Alex's wife. Tears streaked Alma's cheeks.

"Oh, they say there is a terrible fire in the shaft. They say Ike Lewis is in it. And they say—they say my man is in it, too," Alma sobbed, scared about her husband and brother-in-law.

"Oh, it couldn't be so bad as that," Anna said, attempting to comfort Alma. And then she froze. What if Charlie was in the mine? *Oh, God! Surely he wouldn't go down in the fire*, Anna thought. Her apprehension increasing, she ran to the mine.

Meanwhile, in town, Dr. Lyston Howe, the company doctor, saw the smoke. He ran to his office, grabbed his medical bag, and went to the hoisting shaft.

Realizing the fire was worsening, Alex Norberg and John Bundy decided that a small group of rescuers working together would be the most effective way to save lives. This group would go down and assist men to the cages, making as many trips as they could.

Ike Lewis stepped forward immediately.

No 26.
Dr. L.D. Howe one
of the two survivors
who entered the
burning mine at
Cherry Ill. Nov.13,'09

Dr. Lyston Howe

Dr. Howe spoke with Alex Norberg. "Could I be of any [help] down there?"

Norberg thought it was a good idea. Howe could provide emergency care at the bottom, which might help keep suffering men alive until they got into a cage.

Ten men joined Norberg and Bundy's rescue party. Before Norberg joined the others in the cage, he left specific instructions for John Cowley, the hoisting engineer. He told Cowley to pay careful attention to the signal bells that the rescue party would send. The system was very explicit: one bell from the bottom meant hoist the cage; two bells, lower the cage; three bells, men want to come up; four bells, hoist slowly. If Cowley heard one bell and the cage was already moving up or down, it meant *stop the cage*.

In the second vein, the rescue party split into groups to cover more territory.

Dr. Howe walked toward the west. Even though he carried a lantern, Howe couldn't see through the smoke: How would he ever find men who needed him? He made his way cautiously along the roadway, sliding one foot out in front of the other. Suddenly, he kicked something soft. He bent down and felt the object. It was a man! Howe dragged him to the cage and gave him oxygen and medicine to stimulate his circulation. He continued aiding others until the cage was full. Howe squeezed in. He knelt beside the men and treated them as the cage rose. Howe made six trips down into the mine. During one of them, he burned his hand when he used it to smother flames that were burning a miner's clothes.

Meanwhile, Alexander Rosenjack, who had returned to the mine earlier, made a final attempt to connect a hose in the mule stable. He wrapped a wet rag around his mouth and nose and put on a pair of goggles. He tied a rope around his waist, then inched forward into the stable. The men with him saw his clothes begin to smoke and his hair get singed. They grabbed the rope and pulled him back. Blisters covered his hands and face.

Conditions in another area of the second vein had worsened. Assistant mine manager Walter Waite had spent the afternoon working in the northwest area of the second vein. When he first smelled smoke, he thought it might be from a miner's lamp. Or perhaps a cap had caught fire. When the smell still hung in the air minutes later, Waite investigated. The smell got stronger after he walked into a wider passageway. There, he met George Eddy, who told him about the fire. Waite knew they had to alert unaware miners still at work.

"You go this way," Waite said, pointing in one direction. "I'll go that way and tell the men and then we'll meet at the [hoisting shaft] entrance again." Eddy followed Waite's order and alerted every man he saw.

As Waite hurried along the roadway, he heard men shouting "Fire!" Waite helped stumbling men to the main roadway and put them into a cage. One of the rescue party men tried to pull Waite into the cage.

"Let me stay where I am," Waite said. "There are a lot of other fellows who ought to get out of here. . . . I'll try and do what I can." He returned to the passageway that led to the mine's western rooms.

A short time later, a "crowd of panic stricken miners" swept Waite into the main roadway, the one that led toward the hoisting shaft. This time, he saw flames. Realizing that entering the flames meant certain death, Waite shouted, "Stand back from the flame!" But the panicked men didn't listen. Instead, they ran closer. Waite saw them falling one on top of the other, overwhelmed by the smoke.

George Eddy ran into the main roadway and stood beside Waite.

"My God, we'll all die. We've got to get these fellows back," Eddy said. Waite and Eddy sprang in front of another group of men and stopped them. One of the men, miner William Clelland, was relieved to see them. He knew Waite and Eddy had been coal miners for a long time. Their experience and knowledge just might save his life.

ON THE SURFACE
SATURDAY AFTERNOON

By 3:00 p.m., most of Cherry's residents surrounded the mouth of the hoisting shaft. Crying women and children pushed through the crowd. Over and over, the same questions filled the air.

Have you seen my husband?

Are my sons here?

Did my brother get out?

Where is my papa?

Meanwhile, a special train had arrived with Ladd's fire engine and firefighters. They attached hoses to the fire engine and water tanks. They started pumping hundreds of gallons of water down the smoking air shaft. Still, flames burned brightly.

By 3:30 p.m., a thick cloud of dark smoke towered two hundred feet above the mine. Fire crept "nearer and nearer" to the hoisting shaft. Members of the rescue team sat or lay near the mouth of the shaft, taking a few moments for recovery. Many had already made six trips into the mine. Each time they had come to the surface, their clothes were scorched and the insides of their throats were seared by the heat. Smoke had stained their teeth black.

Even though the situation was grim, twelve men—John Bundy,

CHERRY MINE—MOUTH OF SHAFT

The steady stream of men, women, and children soon formed a crowd around the hoisting shaft.

Alex Norberg, and Ike Lewis among them—still had the strength and determination to try one more time. Dr. Howe, who had just come up in a cage with Alexander Rosenjack, tried to join them. John Bundy pushed him away, thinking of the injured men waiting in the mine's small hospital.

"They will need you. . . . No use risking your life down here," said Bundy.

Howe stepped back.

After John Cowley, in the engine house, received the signal from the cager, he lowered the cage. The cable sizzled and whirred as the cage dropped.

When the cage reached the bottom, the cable went slack. Cowley had been told that the rescue party might attempt to bring up men from the third vein using the small emergency cage that sat in the third vein, at the very bottom of the hoisting shaft. If they attempted this, the cable would go slack while they made the connection. Cowley assumed that was happening.

Five minutes passed, then ten.

Cowley listened for signals.

Then three bells rang: men wanted to come up. Cowley started the hoist engine.

Next, Cowley heard four bells. As the signal demanded, he slowed the engine.

Four more bells. Cowley assumed this meant the rescue party had attached the emergency cage and wanted the large cage to move slower so the rope attached to the emergency cage wouldn't snap. So he slowed the engine even more.

One bell. As per the signal, Cowley stopped the engine.

And then, a confusion of signals: three bells . . . four bells . . . one bell . . . two bells . . . six bells . . . seven bells. Cowley had never received a signal of seven bells! What was happening?

Meanwhile, Herbert Lewis and Dr. Howe stood with the cager near the mouth of the hoisting shaft. The strange signals disturbed them. They knew something was wrong.

"Pound on the pipe [that goes down the shaft] and try to get an answer from below," Lewis said to the cager.

The cager pounded the pipe. No answer.

He called down. Still no answer.

Suddenly, the cable holding the cage shook, as if someone was shaking it back and forth. Dr. Howe told the cager that he should signal John Cowley over in the engine house. But the cager hesitated; he hadn't received a clear signal from below to hoist the cage. According to Illinois law, the cager could not let Cowley raise a cage unless someone at the bottom of the mine had signaled the cager to do so.

By then, the cage had been down for close to half an hour. Herbert Lewis feared for his brother Ike. He and Dr. Howe raced from the hoisting shaft to the engine room. Howe begged Cowley to raise the cage. Cowley mumbled a reply.

"Come over [here] . . . look at the hole . . . see the smoke coming out," Howe demanded. "For God's sake, pull that cage away or the men will die."

Still, Cowley hesitated. People by the hoisting shaft pleaded and screamed for someone to raise the cage. Finally, after consulting with several men, Cowley slowly raised the cage.

Standing at the engine house door, Lewis waved his arm, urging Cowley to haul faster. When the charred, smoking cage reached the surface, those within sight gasped.

Four men had left the cage and tried to climb the timber framework. Their burned remains knelt or lay sprawled on top of the cage.

Smoke billowed from the hoisting shaft.
Poor visibility increased the confusion as
rescue efforts began.

Eight men huddled inside the cage. All of them were severely burned. Some of their clothes were on fire.

Herbert Lewis ran to the cage and threw water on one man's clothes. He was told it was John Bundy. Lewis grabbed the leg of another man and pulled him off the cage. Only then did he look at the man's face. It was Ike. Overcome with grief, Herbert knelt beside his brother's body and cried. A friend helped him home.

Dr. Howe checked the men—John Bundy, Alex Norberg, Ike Lewis, everyone—for signs of life. But all twelve were dead.

John Cowley lowered the cages several more times in case other men reached the shaft. Each time, the cages came up empty.

CHAPTER 6
TRAPPED!

More than an hour after lunch, and unaware of the fire, John Lorimer and Thomas White finished drilling a few small holes into the rock in their room, about three quarters of a mile south of the hoisting shaft. As miners in both veins regularly did, they planned to explode some shots at the end of their shift. Lorimer thought he heard mining shots being fired in other rooms. Believing it must be quitting time, Lorimer and White plugged a paper cartridge stuffed with explosive powder into each hole, lit the fuses and headed out.

The buddies had walked about half a mile when they smelled smoke. When they opened a passageway door, they met "smoke in

John Lorimer

volumes" and "knew by the smell that it was timber burning." "It made our eyes smart so that tears ran from them," White recalled.

Flames blocked the way to the air shaft. The hoisting shaft was their only chance for escape. They groped along the main roadway's wall until they reached the hoisting shaft. No cage was there.

John Lorimer grabbed the signal bell's knob handle. The red-hot knob burned Lorimer's fingers, but he didn't let go. He rang three times.

The cage did not descend.

Lorimer wrapped his cap around his hand and rang the bell again. Still no cage.

Coughing from the smoke, White and Lorimer knew that if they didn't move to a place with better air, they would die. They turned back toward the coal rooms, thinking they heard voices.

Almost a mile away to the west, Antenore Quartaroli also thought he heard a shot. It was about 2:45 p.m. Like Lorimer and White, he thought it was quitting time and went to see if others were leaving. When Quartaroli smelled smoke, he ran back for his buddy, Francesco Zanarini. They grabbed their coats and lunch pails and ran for the hoisting shaft. The roadways got hotter and smokier as they neared the shaft. About five hundred feet from the hoisting shaft, they opened one of the roadway doors and went through. The air was so hot, they couldn't breathe. Quartaroli called out, but no one answered.

Weak and dizzy, the buddies dropped their lunch pails and stumbled back through the doors. They hurried toward the air shaft. The flame of Quartaroli's lamp dimmed, but Zanarini's still

Thomas White

burned brightly. Fortunately, they found a gallon can of oil. They filled both lamps and took the can with them. They squeezed past rocks and timbers strewn on the floor.

As they walked along one roadway that led toward the air shaft, Quartaroli heard men speaking in Italian. It was his neighbors, Giacomo and Salvatore Pigati! Salvatore held his coat sleeve over his mouth. From them, Quartaroli learned that the air shaft was aflame. The group tried to approach the hoisting shaft from another direction, but flames blocked them. Within a few minutes, a group of panicked men surrounded them.

Then they heard Walter Waite shout, "Stand back from the flame!"

Quartaroli and his friends gathered around Walter Waite and George Eddy. Everyone's lungs and throat ached from breathing smoke and scorching-hot air. Waite told them to rest, to stay where they were for a few minutes. He and Eddy were going to check one last roadway to the hoisting shaft and would come right back.

The two men hadn't gone far when they saw a pit car blocking the roadway ahead. Before they reached the car, the three mules hitched to it collapsed and died. That dashed their hope of reaching the hoisting shaft that way; clearly the air was bad. Waite turned to Eddy.

"We are caught like rats in a trap. But there is no need to tell the boys about seeing the mules," he said.

Waite and Eddy returned to the group. Waite told the men they would die if they stayed where they were. He said the group should head into the western tunnels, where the smoke had not penetrated. The fresher air there would sustain them until the fire died. They could try to reach the hoisting shaft again then.

The group trudged deeper into the mine. During a short rest, George Eddy heard shouts. He followed the cries and found Thomas White and John Lorimer almost overwhelmed by black damp. He brought them to the group, which then included twenty-one men. The group finally found better air in a tunnel more than half a mile from the hoisting shaft. By then, their mouths were so dry they couldn't lick their parched lips.

Nearly a mile away, in the eastern area of the second vein, Sam and Alfred Howard tried to reach the hoisting shaft from a different direction. Dead mules, dying men, and flames blocked every road-way they tried. Like Waite's group, they finally sought refuge with a group of men in a tunnel that contained better air. They hoped the fire would soon be extinguished.

ON THE SURFACE
SATURDAY

Aboveground, urgent phone calls and telegrams sought help from neighboring towns. Doctors rushed to Cherry in automobiles and in a special railroad car from Ladd. Pharmacists in nearby Spring Valley stripped drugstore shelves of surgical supplies, loaded them into cars, and "hurried them into Cherry at top speed." At the mine, Dr. Howe and another doctor treated and released mildly injured men. They further treated more severely burned miners in a building set up as a temporary hospital.

No one knew how many men were trapped in the mine. The company ordered all miners to report to the office so they could be counted. Meanwhile, even though nightfall approached, hundreds of men, women, and children remained at the mine. Drizzle dampened their coats, shawls, and jackets. Some people cried softly; others sobbed aloud. They were hungry and cold, but they wouldn't leave. Doing so meant giving up hope.

Lena Waite stood among them. Her husband, Walter, was in the mine. Her sister-in-law, Anna Waite, hadn't found Charlie either.

George Eddy's wife, Elizabeth, and their daughters—Florence,

Jennie, and Esther—waited in the crowd. Elizabeth had been napping when George left the house earlier, so he hadn't said goodbye as he usually did. When she first heard news of the fire, Elizabeth wasn't too worried about her husband. She knew he was off duty. Then some men who had escaped told her they had seen George in the mine. Fearful, she and the girls hoped rescuers would soon find him.

Erminia Quartaroli, hugging her infant son, yearned for news of Antenore. The Pigatis, who lived next door, and nearly every wife, mother, sister, and young brother who lived on Erminia's street waited for news of family members still in the mine.

Jessie Love mingled in the crowd. Both of her brothers—Robert and Alexander Deans—had escaped from the mine. When Robert returned home, frightened and shaken, he'd told her that a torch had set hay bales on fire. And that overcome by smoke, he'd been carried to the surface. Now she heard people around her blaming him and Alexander Rosenjack for the fire. But she was most concerned about the whereabouts of her husband, John. He and his three brothers were still in the mine.

Ladd's firefighters continued pumping hundreds of gallons of water down the air shaft, but smoke still poured from both shafts. A mine official telephoned the Chicago Fire Department, even though it was one hundred miles away. Perhaps their experienced firefighters could help.

After nightfall, company officials sealed the mine, hoping that a lack of air would smother the fire. The crowd watched, horrified, as workers covered the hoisting shaft with planks and poured sand on top to fill the cracks. Everyone felt the coal company was abandoning their loved ones. Officials told them that rescue efforts would resume in the morning.

SATURDAY NIGHT
UNDERGROUND

By 7:00 p.m., Waite and Eddy's group had made another attempt to reach the hoisting shaft. Black damp stopped them. The gas was odorless, but miners knew it was there when they took a breath. It felt as though a weight were "crushing the chest," and it made them light-headed. Dizzy from the deadly gas, Antenore Quartaroli felt "as if the earth were whirling." He closed his eyes, stumbled, and fell. He could hardly breathe. His friend William Clelland helped him stand. Everyone encouraged him to keep walking as the group retreated farther west in the mine.

Later that night, stomachs growled. Waite told the men not to eat, since they didn't know when they would get out. He suggested that they pool lunch-pail leftovers and share them. One man hadn't been too hungry at lunch; he contributed four slices of bread, two slices of meat, a pickle, a piece of pie, and some tea. Ruggeri Buonfiglio, a teenager who lived near Quartaroli, said they should kill a mule. No one wanted to do that except as a last resort. Francesco Zanarini, William Clelland, and Buonfiglio scavenged left-behind lunch pails in nearby workstations. They found only one slice of bread and half a bottle of water. They pooled these with the other food. They all hoped they'd be out of the mine before the food ran out. To save oil, the group extinguished all but one lamp.

Everyone knew the situation was dire. In the nearly dark tunnel, John Lorimer drew comfort from a hymn he often sang in church. At first he sang alone: *"Abide with me, fast falls the eventide; the darkness deepens, Lord with me abide."* Clelland and others soon joined in. Even the men who spoke little English began humming the tune. The music sustained them through the night. Waite and Eddy encouraged their companions not to give up hope.

Meanwhile, in a different area of the mine, Sam and Alfred Howard sat with about forty men. Sam didn't know what would happen during the next few hours. Whether he would live or die. But he had things to tell people, especially his mother and his fiancée, Mamie. He pulled a pencil from his pocket and jotted his thoughts on a piece of paper.

> *Alive at 10:30 yet.*
> *10:45. 11:00 sharp. Big Sam D. Howard.*
> *Alfred, my brother is with me yet.*
> *A good many dead mules and men. I tried to save some, but came almost losing myself.*
> *If I am dead give my diamond ring to Mamie Robinson. The ring is at the post office. I had it sent there.*

The only thing I regret is my brother [who] could help mother out after I am dead and gone. I tried my best to get out, but could not. . . .

It is five minutes past 11 o'clock and the air is fine, but sometimes it is so bad it almost puts a fellow's life out. . . .

To keep me from thinking I thought I would write these few lines.

There is rock falling all over. We have our buckets full of water . . . and we drink it and bathe our heads with it.

CHAPTER 7
BLACK DAMP

Sam Howard's chest felt heavy; he needed more air. He reached for his pencil.

3 o'clock [a.m.] and poor air and black damp.

Sam, Alfred, and their companions fled to another passageway.

4:15 o'clock. Change of place. No black damp, but poor air. We lost a couple of our group. Two men tried to get out and could not get back.
   7:50 o'clock tired, hungry, and sleepy.

Almost a mile to the west, Antenore Quartaroli felt as tired as if he'd walked one hundred miles. He'd tossed and turned all night, unable to sleep.

About 5:00 a.m., Walter Waite asked if anyone had a pencil or some paper. He suggested that everyone write a last goodbye to their families or a friend, just in case they didn't survive. Rescuers would find their notes. William Clelland offered a pencil and a small notebook. Another man had a pencil and some paper too.

Thomas White wrote to his wife:

> I know Maggie you will be in an awful
> state. I have been thinking of you Mag
> and the children. I loved my children and
> wife. But if it is Gods wish for us to go,
> God knows what is best. It is five o'clock
> Sunday morning when I am writing. . . .
> Good-Bye wife and children, be good to the
> children Maggie.
>
> best wishes . . . from your Loving Husband
> Tom White

A discouraged John Lorimer wrote to his wife:

> We have poor hope as the black damp is
> getting the best of us.

George Eddy thought of his three daughters:

I have tried to get out twice but was driven back [by black damp]. Their seams [sic] to be no hope for us, I come down this shaft yesterday to help save the mens lives. I hope the men I got out was saved. . . . Keep Esther and Florence and Jennie together as much as you can.

Black damp muddled their thoughts. Fresh air wasn't flowing into the mine anymore and Eddy realized the shafts had been sealed. The group spent the rest of the morning searching for an area with better air, the stronger men supporting the weak.

As they searched, they discussed how terrible the men on the surface must have felt to seal the shafts. After they reached a safer place, Waite wrote a note on the back of George Eddy's letter. It stated that they didn't blame anyone for the accident and believed everybody was doing everything in their power to rescue them. With everyone's approval, Waite signed every man's name.

In a northeast tunnel, Sam Howard added to his diary.

12 after 8 o'clock on Sunday morning. There is no air. We fanned ourselves with lids of our buckets.
25 after 9 . . . black damp coming both ways.

25 after 10. . . . We gave up all hope. . . . The fan better start above soon. . . .

It is 11 a.m. . . . We are still alive. The only hope is the fan. . . . I won't have strength to write pretty soon.

One of Sam's companions had a life-saving idea: build their own fan with materials they could scavenge!

With renewed hope, Sam grabbed his pencil:

15 after 12 p.m. Sunday. We are having a swell time making fans. If they can't give us air we will make some ourselves. This is the best we can do. We take our turn [cranking] at the fan. We have three of them going.

27 to 3 p.m. and the black damp is coming in on us. Only for the fans we would be dead.

ON THE SURFACE
SUNDAY

Hours before dawn, officials of the St. Paul Coal Company boarded a special train from Chicago. Doctors joined them. Nurses from the Visiting Nurse Association of Chicago sorted through medical supplies as the train steamed toward Cherry.

Illinois's ten state mine inspectors were also en route to Cherry. Even though only one of them had been inside Cherry Mine, they had been ordered to lead the rescue efforts.

Before morning's end, mining engineer Professor Robert Williams and his assistant, James Webb, mine safety experts from a rescue station at the University of Illinois in Champaign, were bringing oxygen tanks and helmets. Experts from other parts of the country would join them soon in Cherry.

Sunday morning newspapers carried the story nationwide. The *Chicago Daily Tribune* headline blared, "Mine on Fire Entombs 391." The *New York Times* reported "400 Caught in Mine; All Believed Dead."

Worried family members remained outside the mine regardless of the weather or time of day.

As the morning passed, the situation in Cherry became chaotic. Men, women, and children continued their vigil at the hoisting shaft. Newspaper reporters asked questions. Photographers set up cameras. Gawkers began arriving in horse-drawn buggies, in automobiles, and on the interurban, an electric trolley that ran to Ladd. They crowded the grocery stores and emptied the shelves for their lunches and dinners.

Coal company clerks visited all of Cherry's dwellings. They wrote down the names of any coal company employees who lived in each place. Two hundred and fifty-six men were still missing.

Inside the mine office, Robert Williams and James Webb told the officials and inspectors the best rescue plan would be to remove trapped miners through the air shaft if it was smoke-free.

Outside the office, angry miners paced. Time was running out for their friends in the mine. After the inspectors announced the plan, the miners quickly tore the planks off the air shaft and chopped away the shaft's concrete cap.

When no smoke appeared, carpenters built the framework for a simple cage. Someone found a huge bucket, big enough that two or three men could share, but only if each man put just one foot inside. Workers fastened a cable to the bucket, threaded it through the hoist, and attached it to the winding wheel in the air shaft's engine house.

Robert Williams attached a wire to a thermometer and lowered it several hundred feet into the air shaft. The temperature was 68°F to 76°F (20°C to 24°C). He lowered and raised a metal bucket. It didn't feel hot. Rescuers could enter the air shaft.

Horses and buggies created a traffic nightmare as Cherry's streets filled with out-of-town volunteers and gawkers.

More than a dozen men volunteered. Dr. Howe examined each of them, making sure they had no trouble breathing. He chose the two healthiest: miners James Hand and Henry Smith. Neither one worked in Cherry. They'd come from nearby towns but were willing to risk their lives for strangers in need. They would work in combination with the safety inspectors during the rescue attempts.

Before Hand and Smith could enter the mine, Robert Williams and James Webb taught them about the rescue equipment. They settled helmets on Hand and Smith's heads and strapped oxygen tanks to their backs. They taught them how to breathe and move

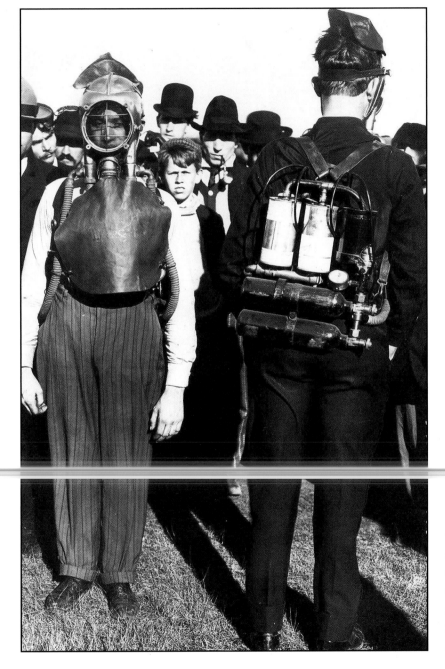

Oxygen tanks and helmets were heavy and unwieldy, but entering the burning mine without them would mean certain death.

safely while wearing the forty-pound equipment. Only then were they ready to attempt a rescue. Inspector James Taylor also suited up and prepared to join the rescue efforts.

At 1:20 p.m., Williams and Smith descended in the bucket. A rope attached to the bucket was their lifeline. They would pull it as the signal to raise the bucket. Each held an electric lamp. At the last moment, someone handed Williams an automobile horn. In those days, the horn was not built into a car's steering wheel. It hung outside the car. When a driver squeezed the horn's rubber ball, the horn honked. Williams would honk the horn rather than pulling the rope. No one could miss its loud sound.

Riding in the bucket was like walking a tightrope. One false move and they would overbalance and fall down the shaft.

The bucket went down.

The crowd waited tensely.

Suddenly, the horn honked. Immediately, the engineer hoisted the bucket. The bucket had become unbalanced. A third man joined them to balance the bucket.

The second time they descended, the bucket dropped three hundred feet before they honked the horn. This time, the bucket had bumped into an obstacle.

On the third try, about 5:00 p.m., Williams, Webb, and Inspector Taylor reached the second vein. But the bucket swung freely in the shaft. There was no landing platform; flames had destroyed it.

Fifteen minutes later, the men returned to the surface. Taylor reported they could only see a distance of about ten feet. Crumbled ceiling rock partially filled the roadway toward the mule stable. But he had some encouraging news. The temperature was only about 68°F (20°C) at the depth where the landing had been. Taylor thought if it remained that way throughout the second vein, miners trapped below might have a chance.

Workers resealed the air shaft at about 11:00 p.m. Williams announced they would make another rescue attempt early Monday morning, this time in the hoisting shaft.

Very late that night, a farmer raced to the mine. He swore he heard shots—the sound of dynamite blasts—under the ground on his farm. Miners were sending signals, he claimed. Hopes rose that Monday would bring good news.

SUNDAY AFTERNOON AND EVENING
UNDERGROUND

Salvatore Pigati wound his pocket watch. He didn't want to lose track of the time or the day. His companions periodically asked what time it was.

At 1:30 p.m., Waite's group—searching yet again for a safer place—stopped to rest. Antenore Quartaroli took his turn with pencil and paper and wrote to his wife, Erminia:

> I am hungry but what disturbs me most is thirst . . . educate our son the best you can, and when he is grown up you tell him

that he had an honest father. I should tell you "rivederci" but I can only tell you "good-bye" forever. A kiss, Antenore

About 5:00 p.m., the group entered a room, or chamber, about three-fourths of a mile west of the air shaft. The air was much clearer. One of the men, a recent immigrant from France, decided to try again for the air shaft. He returned half an hour later, scarcely able to walk. Waite spoke with him, but the man understood very little English. Giacomo Pigati, who spoke some French, told Waite that black damp had blocked their companion's way. That quashed all hope of escape via that route.

As the evening passed, the Frenchman weakened. Giacomo and Salvatore Pigati carried him farther inside the chamber, where the air was somewhat better. Quartaroli wet the man's lips with water and fanned him with his cap. But the man died a few minutes later. They put his body in a sheltered place just inside the chamber's entry.

Late that night, there was still plenty of air in the chamber, but Eddy and some of the men were becoming disoriented. Traces of black damp were creeping in. Waite realized they had to barricade each end of their chamber to block the black damp.

The men knew they were fighting for their lives. They scavenged tools from nearby workstations. They chopped rock from the walls, and with their hands shoveled coal and gravel from the floor. They built two thick barricades that walled their chamber from the rest of

G. PIGATI
BURRIED 8 DAYS
ALIVE CHERRY
MINE DISASTER
PHOTO BY HUGHES
SPRING VALLEY ILL

Giacomo Pigati

the mine. Weakened by lack of air and sleep, several of the exhausted men fainted. The rest determinedly chinked cracks and holes with damp coal dust and clay scraped from the floor. Two hours later, the walls were as airtight as they could make them. George Eddy was so tired that he lay on the floor and immediately fell asleep.

With the barricades completed, their safe chamber was about three hundred feet long and twelve feet wide. The ceiling was so low that only a few of the men could stand completely upright. Still, they lit only one lamp. Now it wasn't to save oil but to preserve the chamber's cold, damp air. A flame needs oxygen to keep burning. (And while it is burning, it produces toxic carbon dioxide gas.) Everyone knew their survival depended on conserving oxygen, even the small amount any extra flames would consume.

John Lorimer and William Clelland again led the men in prayer. They sang hymns. Bone-tired, Thomas White paced the length of the chamber to keep warm. Ruggeri Buonfiglio, Giacomo and Salvatore Pigati, and Quartaroli lay down to sleep, wrapping their arms around one another to share body warmth.

In another area of the mine on Sunday afternoon, the air turned bad where Sam Howard, his brother, and their companions sheltered. Shortly before 4:00 p.m., Sam wrote in his diary that they were "Dying for the want of air."

Sam, Alfred, and the others tried again to reach the hoisting shaft.

20 after 6 p.m. Now we are trying to make the bottom with the fans. We have six of them [fans] moving.

The men traveled along the roadway by leapfrogging the fans in "jumps" that kept the fans about fifteen feet apart. Two hours later, smoke, heat, and black damp forced them to retreat.

15 and 9 p.m. Sunday. Still alive. We had to come back with our fans. . . . We can't move forward or backward.

Sam and Alfred cranked a fan whenever it was their turn. Desperately, they prayed for rescue.

We can stand it with our fans until Monday morning.

CHAPTER 8
COLD, HUNGRY, WEAK, SICK

MONDAY, NOVEMBER 15: DAY 3
UNDERGROUND

Sam Howard could barely concentrate. Black damp had filtered into their tunnel. Some of his companions had died.

> *15 after 2 a.m. Monday. We are cold, hungry, weak, sick . . . Alfred Howard is still alive.*
> *9:15 a.m. Monday morning. Still breathing. Something better turn up or we will soon be gone.*

A few hours later, Sam struggled to remain conscious. His hand felt heavy as lead. So heavy that when he wrote, the pencil's point tore the paper. His letters scrawled, uneven and indistinct.

16 to 1 p.m. Monday. The lives are going out.
I think this is our last. We are getting weak,
Alfred Howard as well as all of us.

Sam and Alfred Howard, and all of their companions, died soon after.

Earlier that same morning, a mile to the west, Salvatore Pigati looked at his watch. It was 7:00 a.m.

"It is time for breakfast," he announced. His companions groaned.

At 11:00 a.m., he said, "It is time for lunch."

Antenore Quartaroli's mouth watered. *There is nothing to eat but hunger*, he thought.

Walter Waite said they could live a few days without food, but they had to find water. Their only hope for water lay within the mine's floor. They searched the lowest areas in their chamber. One man found a damp spot. He grabbed a pick and dug a hole in the clay floor. His thirsty companions gathered and waited.

Slowly, slowly, slowly, groundwater seeped through the coal and gravel.

"We all gave a little cheer when we saw it," Waite recalled.

There was only enough for each man to have a swallow or two. The water was dirty. It stank. With each swallow, tiny particles of coal stuck in their throats. But every man drank it anyway.

At 5:30 Monday morning, workers cleared the top of the hoisting shaft. By 9:00 a.m., Robert Williams and a state inspector descended in a cage. Both wore helmets and carried electric lights; one carried the automobile horn emergency signal.

Smoke blinded them in the second vein, but they shuffled east along the main roadway for about twenty-five feet. Williams didn't see any bodies. He hoped that meant miners might be alive deeper in the mine. After ten minutes, they returned to the surface.

An hour and a half later, James Webb and James Taylor explored the second vein to the west. Conditions there were equally smoky. They turned back after 150 feet.

Until the air cleared, a rescue mission was impossible. Taylor said he had not seen any bodies. But most people didn't believe him. Miners who had escaped said they had climbed over dead men lying in the roadways.

While the inspectors decided what to do next, the sheriff from nearby Princeton swore in extra deputies. By then, thousands of people surrounded the mine and filled Cherry's streets. Cherry's mayor had requested the sheriff's help with crowd control. The mayor feared rescuers would bring up a great many bodies that day. If a grief-stricken crowd lost control, bystanders might get hurt. The mayor ordered all saloons closed for the day. He didn't want liquor fueling anyone's anger.

The mayor wasn't the only man worried about safety. Alexander Rosenjack and hoisting engineer John Cowley were worried too. People blamed them for the fire and for the rescue party's deaths. One man later testified that Rosenjack spoke to him on Monday morning. According to him, Rosenjack said, "I am getting scared here. The [men in town] have threatened me." He suggested Rosenjack speak with a lawyer who worked for the state of Illinois.

The Bureau County coroner, an official who investigates unusual deaths, had started an inquiry to discover what caused the fire and the resulting loss of life. He planned to question many people. The lawyer knew the coroner had already questioned Cowley. Afterward, the sheriff had placed a guard on Cowley. But the coroner intended to question Rosenjack too. When the lawyer heard that threats had been made against Rosenjack, he suggested that Rosenjack hide. He told Rosenjack to report in every day or so until the coroner needed his testimony. Rosenjack agreed.

Late Monday afternoon, workers repaired the huge fan above the air shaft and blew air into the mine. Rescuers Williams and Webb descended for a third rescue attempt via the hoisting shaft. When the cage reached the second vein, they discovered that the air current had cleared some of the smoke. But they hadn't gone far before they saw fire. The current had also fanned embers into flame! They raced back to the cage and honked the automobile horn to raise the cage. Even as the cage rose, they honked it again. Raise the cage faster!

Hearing news of the flames, the Ladd firefighters connected a hose to a railroad tank car filled with water. Williams and Webb dragged the hose into the cage and returned to the second vein. On the bottom, they aimed the hose at the fire, but only a weak stream of water flowed out. Something was broken. By the time they surfaced and found the cause, the flames had spread. Wall and ceiling timbers had cracked, and sections of the ceiling had collapsed. The collapse made so much noise that people on the surface heard it.

After a short discussion, the inspectors and mine safety engineers agreed that the mine was too dangerous for a fourth rescue attempt on Monday. They turned off the fan and resealed the hoisting shaft.

The families and friends of missing miners cried out when they realized there was no further hope for rescue that day.

WORRIES

Every woman worried for her loved ones trapped below. But the women had other worries as well. Without the twice-monthly wages their men—and boys—earned, the family would have no income. How would they pay for food, shelter, and clothes? They needed money.

Earlier in the day, women had stood in a long line, some cradling infants in their arms, and waited at the mine office to receive a pay voucher. The company's bookkeeper said that when one young woman reached the window, she demanded in Italian, "Give me back my husband. I don't want this money. Give me back my husband."

MISS MABEL MORLOCK — MRS PEARL RINGLAND — MISS CATHEHERINE GARSIDE
MISS MAUDE M? GINNIS — MISS CORA HAWSAN — MISS GERTRUDE GILPIN

*Nurses from the Visiting Nurse Association of Chicago were among the first
responders to the disaster. They packed medical supplies and quickly boarded
the relief train to Cherry.*

Early Monday morning, nurse Pearl Ringland, aided by one of the six nurses who had arrived with her the night before, began caring for injured men in the hospital that had been hastily set up in a railroad car. Ringland and Dr. Howe realized that miners' families desperately needed help. She tasked her remaining nurses with visiting every miner's home to treat ill women and children. Their reports concerned Ringland.

"During the day the uneasiness seems to have increased among the families and it has been difficult to keep them in their houses. Women with babies in arms walked through the rain to the mine shaft as early as 5 o'clock, many of the children wearing worn-out shoes and summer clothing," she learned.

Ringland entered several homes in response to her nurses' concerns.

"The mother with her three little ones was sitting in a cold room and no food. . . . Another home I visited where the mother was ill and five children, the oldest 8 years of age, were crying because 'pa' did not come home. . . . Never have I witnessed such utter grief and hopelessness," she said later.

Meanwhile, at three funeral services, friends offered words of sympathy to three grieving families whose loved ones had burned to death in and on top of the hoisting cage on Saturday afternoon. One of the dead was a fifteen-year-old boy who had joined the ill-fated rescue party to find his father, who was still below. A procession of crying mourners followed each horse-pulled hearse as it rolled down Main Street and turned toward the cemetery.

HELP

Many strangers came to Cherry and volunteered their help. The coal company sent railroad cars to be used as sleeping quarters and dining rooms for the volunteers.

Ernest Bicknell, the national director of the American Red Cross, arrived in Cherry and became chairperson of the Cherry Relief Committee. The committee's goal was to quickly help bereaved families. The seven men on the committee oversaw the aid—food, clothing, shelter, and money—given to miners' families.

Volunteers set up a warehouse in downtown Cherry. There, organized teams stored donations that were shipped in on railroad cars or came from nearby towns. Men rode horseback to the surrounding farms. They asked farmers to donate food. The farmers gave generously. They filled wagons with vegetables, hams, bacon, and beef and drove to Cherry. Some tucked in meals cooked and ready to eat. They deposited the food at the warehouse. Volunteers distributed goods from the warehouse to the families in need. Distributing the supplies from one place avoided confusion and waste.

The *Chicago Daily Tribune*'s readers were horrified to read of the disaster. They wanted to help suffering families. Responding to their concern, the newspaper established a relief fund. Donations would be immediately forwarded to the American Red Cross for Cherry's families. As of Monday evening, the fund had collected almost $1,500.

For efficient distribution, donations of food and clothing were stored in a building in downtown Cherry that served as a temporary warehouse.

DAY'S END

By 7:00 Monday evening, both shafts had been resealed. The superintendent of the mine, James Steele, and the safety experts had agreed that the firefighters had to get the fire under control before any more rescue attempts were made. They planned

to investigate the shafts again in the morning and plan further afterward.

Desperate to rescue trapped friends and relatives, some miners offered to enter the mine regardless of the fire. Under this pressure, Steele announced grim news. Robert Williams had told him that many bodies lay near the hoisting shaft. Williams had not publicly announced the news because he thought the crowd would panic and people might get hurt. Sadly, Steele's admission merely confirmed what many people already suspected.

That evening at home, Nellie Lorimer hoped her husband, John, was alive. For the past two nights, she had prayed for his safety. With the mine shafts sealed, she no longer expected to see him alive. She had decided it "would be asking too much to pray to God for his life." She prayed only that his body would be recovered, so she could bury it.

Worries flooded Jessie Love. Her husband and brothers-in-law were still in the mine. Now her brother Robert Deans was gone. Earlier, a man—an "official from the shaft"—had come to her house and spoken with him. Within minutes, Robert wrapped a scarf around his face and went with the man. They climbed into a green automobile and left town. Afterward, Jessie went to the mine office. All the company clerk would tell her was that Robert had been taken to a town about ten miles away; he would be back later that night or in the morning. Still, Jessie worried. She was in charge of all the family's money: she knew that Robert didn't have any.

Salvatore Pigati finally took his turn with the pencil at 7:00 p.m. Scared that he would never get out of the mine, the unmarried man wrote, in Italian, to Giacomo's wife:

> Dear Sister-in-law,
>
> There is no hope that I will come out, up until now we are like rats in a trap. . . . Write to my bereaved parents and tell them about our end . . . have me buried beside my brother as we will unfortunately have the same death. . . .
>
> With tears in my eyes. . . .
> Your affectionate brother-in-law
> Salvatore Pigati

CHAPTER 9
EATING SUNSHINE

Water from the hole in the floor the previous day had temporarily slaked Antenore Quartaroli's thirst. But the water was so bad that he and the others soon felt sick to their stomach. They had to find another source.

During the night, Walter Waite had felt up and down the chamber walls. Finally, he found a few drops of water trickling from a crack. He hollowed out five shallow holes along the base of the crack. The men divided themselves into five groups and assigned each group a certain hole. To make sure every man got water, they set up a drinking order. On his turn, Quartaroli sucked in water until the hole was empty. He licked the bottom of the hole for every last drop. He estimated that the hole held less than a cup of water. The slimy water contained rock grains and tasted nasty, but he was grateful to have it.

The men searched farther away for more damp cracks. They even pounded the walls to make more cracks. If water seeped out, they stuffed a scrap of material torn from a shirt into the crack. When water soaked into the material, a man chewed the scrap until he had squeezed out every drop.

Small drinks calmed Quartaroli's thirst but not his hunger pangs. They'd had no food for three days. At first, they ate sunshine, the paraffin that fueled their lamps. Warmed inside the miners' mouths, the hard wax softened so they could chew it, like gum. After a while, they swallowed it. It took the edge off hunger pangs, but not for long. They chewed on other things, such as pipe tobacco.

Near noontime, their last remaining lamp flickered. It still contained fuel, but the amount of oxygen in the chamber's air had become so low that it could barely sustain the flame. The chamber was almost completely dark; only the tiniest flame saved them from darkness. In the dimmest of light, Giacomo Pigati held a piece of paper he normally filled with explosive powder for a shot. He wrote to his wife, Rosalie:

This is the fourth day we have been down here. I am writing this in the dark because we have been eating the wax from our safety lamps. I also have eaten a plug of tobacco, some bark [from the timbers], and some of my shoe. I could only chew it. . . . I am not afraid to die . . . I think my time has come. . . . You have been a good wife. . . . It has been very quiet down here and I wonder what has become of our comrades. Good-by [sic], until heaven shall bring us together.

The lamp's tiny flame guttered. It flickered and went out.

Someone struck a match, then another. Each time, the flame flickered and died.

And then . . . total darkness.

Darkness so complete that it made no difference whether John Lorimer had his eyes open or closed.

Darkness so complete that it wrapped them like a second skin.

Ruggeri Buonfiglio sobbed and cried out in Italian.

Quartaroli's heart raced; Cherry Mine was his tomb.

For four days, a small, glimmering flame had bound them together. They could see each other's faces. Now, all at once, every man was blind. In that terrifying moment, each man felt alone.

During the night, Ladd's firefighters fed one end of a two-and-a-half-inch canvas hose in through a hole at the top of the hoisting shaft. It sprayed eighty gallons of water a minute. Still not enough to quench the fire. Fortunately, more powerful equipment was on the way.

At 2:30 a.m., a special train, sent by the Chicago, Milwaukee, and St. Paul Railroad, left Chicago in a burst of steam. Its locomotive pulled eight cars. Five were tank cars, each containing ten thousand gallons of water. A fire engine and firefighting apparatus filled the sixth car. Chicago fire chief James Horan's crew had loaded it with five thousand feet of hose, thirty-six handheld fire extinguishers, and iron pipes for transporting water. Six firefighters hopped on board. Minutes before the train chugged away from the depot, railroad workers attached three more cars. The seventh car contained two thousand additional feet of fire hose, just shipped from Minnesota. The eighth and ninth cars held food, clothing, and 250 pine coffins.

Tuesday morning dawned windy, wet, and cold. Midmorning, miners clustered outside the mine briefly left their posts to join the rest of Cherry's miners at the funeral services for Ike Lewis and Alex Norberg. Rain drenched hundreds of mourners, as if the sky cried with them. Church bells tolled throughout the day as the remains of six more of Saturday's ill-fated rescue party were laid to rest in Cherry's cemetery or sent to nearby towns for services and burial. Only one body still lay in the temporary morgue. That miner's family had not yet arrived to claim his remains.

Hours earlier, long before daybreak, Cherry Mine's payroll— $19,000 in cash—had arrived from the St. Paul Coal Company. Tuesday morning, the bookkeeper reopened the mine office's pay window and traded cash for the pay vouchers given to the women on Monday.

Family and friends accompany a hearse on its way to Cherry's cemetery. The funerals for the twelve heroes who died on and in the burning cage were the first of many in the following weeks and months.

At noon, workers broke the hoisting shaft's seal. Smoke curled out. An inspector hung four thermometers in the shaft. Their temperatures ranged from 110°F to 115°F (43°C to 46°C)—too hot for helmeted men to safely enter the mine. Inspectors would take more temperature readings throughout the day. But as long as the temperature remained that hot, they would not risk the lives of rescue teams.

While mourners attended afternoon funeral services, Chicago's firefighters pulled their engine to the mine. They connected a four-inch hose to the engine's pump. Hand over hand, they lowered one end into the hoisting shaft. Water gushed into the shaft at five

Chicago's fire department sent one of its engines to Cherry.

hundred to six hundred gallons per minute. They let the hose run, full blast, until very late that night.

On Tuesday, downtown stores owned by the St. Paul Coal Company dispensed goods without charge to families in need.

The Cherry Relief Committee and the Salvation Army organized donated goods in the warehouse and reached out to families. The *Chicago Daily Tribune*'s relief fund had swelled to more than $5,000. The donations came from churches, businesses, and individual people.

Ladd's firefighters welcomed the assistance of the firefighters from Chicago. The much larger hose they brought with them spewed more gallons of water per minute into the mine than the hose previously used.

Meanwhile, the crowd at the mine grew more frustrated. The president of the United Mine Workers of Illinois spoke with company officials. He told them many miners were willing to enter the mine to find the 256 men listed as missing. He said the union would assume responsibility for their lives. But the inspectors refused.

Officials worried that miners and angry families might riot. Concerned about this possibility, Illinois's governor ordered two companies of the Illinois National Guard to go to Cherry.

In town, nurses continued their work. Maude McGinnis, one of Pearl Ringland's nurses, spent the day consoling women and children. In the afternoon, two women, speaking in a mixture of English and Lithuanian, asked her to come with them to their friend's house. She was pregnant and needed help.

McGinnis sent for a doctor. The baby was born shortly before midnight. McGinnis's heart ached.

"In this cottage where all should have been happiness in honor of the newborn sat three widows grieving for their loved ones," she said. She admired the women, who, despite their own heartbreaking losses, had the strength to support their friend.

A short time later, McGinnis entered John Love's home. She comforted Jessie and her children. The Love family wasn't the only despairing family on Steele Street. Of the street's row of thirty-three identical houses, most of the men and boys who lived in thirty of the homes were still missing. Two of the Loves' Steele Street neighbors—members of Saturday's rescue party—had been buried that afternoon.

CHAPTER 10
ARE YOU ASLEEP?

By sunrise Wednesday, two state militia companies reached Cherry to help control the crowd. Their captains stationed them in three places: a ring encircling the train cars that housed the doctors, nurses, reporters, safety experts, and mine officials; the area around the mine shafts; and Cherry's business district.

Consuls who represented the governments of Italy, Russia, Germany, Austria, and France arrived and offered assistance to emigrants from their countries. On Wednesday afternoon, the representative from the Italian consulate in Chicago visited the homes of Italian miners. What he learned saddened him.

National Guard members stood at the train cars that housed nurses, doctors, and other volunteers to protect them from harassment by those who might distract or disturb them as they attended to their assigned duties.

"One poor Italian woman told me that her husband and three sons were in the mine. She is all alone and has no friends or relatives," he reported. "She has wept until she is ill. . . . My government has given orders that any woman or family that wishes to return to Italy may do so at our country's expense. I told all of them this and they refused to leave. They declared that they wanted to stay in America." Regardless of the hardships they might face, the United States was their home.

In the mine office, state mine inspectors conferred most of the day. Except for the hole made for the firefighters' hoses, the hoisting shaft remained sealed. It was too hot for entry.

A thermometer in the air shaft, however, showed a nearly normal temperature. Although the air quality was poor—it quickly snuffed a lamp's flame—if investigators wore a helmet and an oxygen tank, they should be safe.

That evening, safety expert Robert Williams and another man got into the small bucket and were tied in place so the bucket wouldn't tip. The bucket was lowered until the men could peer into the passageway near the air shaft. Since the men's helmets were rigidly fixed in place, neither man could turn his head without turning his whole body. After a quick look, they signaled to raise the bucket.

When Williams surfaced, he tried to offer hope to the miners who surrounded him. "There is a great deal of gas down there and it appears that there has been a cave-in. . . . However, the conditions are good for a genuine attempt at rescue tomorrow." He reported that properly equipped firefighters could descend in the morning and

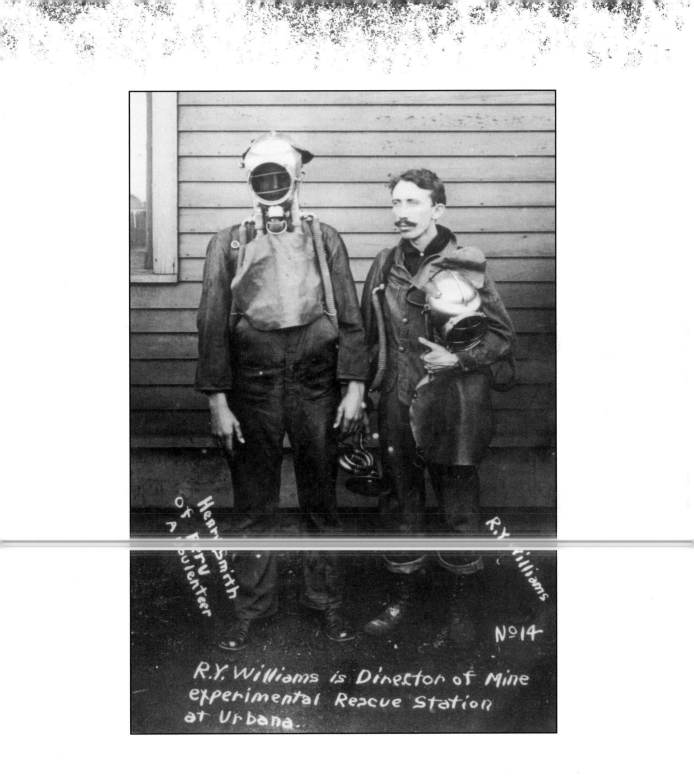

Henry Smith
of Peru
A Voulenteer

R.Y. Williams

Nº14

R.Y. Williams is Director of Mine experimental Rescue Station at Urbana.

hose the fire. But not in the small bucket. It was too hazardous. To work efficiently, they needed a larger free-hanging cage they could easily enter and exit.

To help them do this, George Rice, a mining engineer and expert from the United States Geological Survey, spent Wednesday night and Thursday morning supervising carpenters as they built a small hoisting tower and a free-hanging cage.

Wearing helmets and other protective clothing made it impossible for rescuers to turn their heads or move quickly. But gases, smoke, and falling debris made the protective gear essential. Bags and tanks contained oxygen to sustain the rescuers.

Salvatore Pigati and William Clelland broke the glass face off their pocket watches. Now they could feel the position of the hour and minute hands. Without light, it was the only way to know the time.

In the total darkness, time seemed suspended. Nobody knew how long they'd slept, or even if they had. Feeling the watch hands was the only way Pigati and Clelland could assure their companions that hours had indeed passed. It was how they kept track of what day it was.

Walter Waite did his best to ease their despair. Every so often, he called each man by name. He asked each one: "Are you asleep? How are you feeling? How are you getting along?"

Hearing each other answer gave most of them hope. But someone answered that they'd be better off if they died. Waite urged everyone to think of their family. To hang on to life so they could hold their loved ones again.

One of the young men from Lithuania cheered himself by whistling. Endlessly. Eventually, it "jarred every one's nerves."

"You can stop that!" his companions called.

He did, but he whistled again later.

Once, George Eddy attempted to reach the tiny water hole for his turn to drink. His legs felt so heavy that he couldn't walk. Ruggeri Buonfiglio took Eddy's arm and helped him to the small hole.

"Don't feel bad—we get out and then I will get you wine to drink,"

Buonfiglio promised. Both men hoped they would live long enough for his words to come true.

Antenore Quartaroli's arms and legs were sluggish. His buddy, Francesco Zanarini, was even weaker, as was a miner named Daniel Holofzak. At forty-five years old, Holofzak was the oldest man in the group. He suffered from asthma and wheezed with every breath. Holofzak especially needed more water. But the chamber's water holes were nearly dry. The men licked the damp walls, but it didn't satisfy their thirst.

Quartaroli and two others decided to search again within the chamber for water. Quartaroli's bones creaked when he stood. He could hardly walk. Keeping one hand on the wall, shuffling so they wouldn't trip and fall, the three slowly moved farther along the chamber. The group had only one pick, which the three men took with them. Lifting it to dig small holes took all of their energy. Very little water seeped in. But it was better than nothing. Everyone could have a small sip.

From time to time, Walter Waite or William Clelland poked the pick's point through one of the barricades and sniffed, hoping to smell fresh air. That would mean the shafts were open. That rescue might be coming. On that day, they sensed no current and quickly resealed the hole.

Salvatore Pigati pulled his watch from his pocket. He felt the time and shared it. They figured it was probably Wednesday night. In small groups, they lay close together and tried to sleep. Ruggeri Buonfiglio sobbed and cried that he wanted to be with his mother, father, and brothers. George Eddy comforted him as best he could.

CHAPTER 11

A PECULIAR BUTTON

George Eddy could not get comfortable. When he lay on his back, bumps in the floor poked his spine. If he rolled to his side, they poked his hips.

After what seemed like forever, it was his turn to drink. Too weak to stand, Eddy crawled along the floor, feeling his way to the water hole where he was supposed to go for water. When his fingers found its rim, he pushed his cracked lips into the hole to suck in the swallow or two that had accumulated since his last drink hours ago. The hole was empty. Someone had sneaked to the hole out of turn and drunk the water.

Eddy was furious. He yelled that someone was stealing water, and that if he found out who it was, he would kill him. Whoever had broken the group's pact of taking turns was, in effect, stealing another man's chance of survival. After that, Eddy set up a rotating guard at the water holes so no one could sneak an extra turn.

One man wanted to tear down a barricade and head for the main shaft. Waite knew the black damp was still too strong and would quickly overcome anyone who left. Everyone argued with the man until he finally agreed to stay.

The awful theft of water and the man's strong desire to break down the barricade made the men realize how important it was to stick together as a band. Those who had some strength sat beside the weakest—Ruggeri Buonfiglio, Daniel Holofzak, and a Belgian miner named Leopold Dumont—and urged them not to give up. They told them help was on its way.

And prayed that it was true.

ON THE SURFACE
THURSDAY

As they had for the past five days, families crowded around the mine Thursday morning. Carpenters completed work on the free-hanging cage for the air shaft. Hopes rose that rescuers would enter the mine soon.

In the early afternoon, workers broke a hole in the air shaft's concrete cap just big enough for the free-hanging cage. The inspectors feared that a large hole would let too much air into the mine and refuel the fire. George Rice, Robert Williams, and another man donned helmets and oxygen tanks and descended to the second vein. They carried the automobile horn to signal the surface.

The air was much clearer; only a smoky haze still clung to the ceiling. In one direction, a cave-in completely blocked the passageway. They walked a short distance in the other direction and found a miner's body. More bodies lay farther along the roadway. They inspected conditions in the second vein for about half an hour and returned to the surface.

They described what they'd seen. The timbers that lined the air shaft were charred, but firefighters and others could work there safely. Before any of them went down, three inspectors retrieved the closest miner's body, which they covered with canvas.

Later that afternoon, miners also opened the hoisting shaft. Chicago firefighters sprayed the shaft with thousands of gallons of water. It sheeted from the timbers that lined the shaft and flooded the bottom. The inspectors planned to restart the fan that evening. They hoped soggy timbers and large puddles on the floor would prevent flare-ups when the current of fresh air entered the mine.

As the evening wore on, fresh air and hose water cooled the hoisting shaft. Finally it was safe enough for firefighters to go down the hoisting shaft. They blasted small remaining flames with a steady stream of water, but their battle was far from over. Embers

Men standing on top of the temporary framework installed
above the air shaft prepared to monitor the inspectors' descent.
The metal tank of Chicago's fire engine is just visible beyond
the crowd clustered in the center of the photograph.

hid beneath debris and within timbers. The coal vein posed a hazard too. It could catch fire if it came into contact with embers or flames. All night, the firefighters worked in shifts to prevent new outbreaks.

The mine inspectors worried about black damp. Since they could safely run the fan only at a low speed, the poisonous gas remained strong in the mine. They hoped the level of black damp would drop during the night.

While the firefighters and mine inspectors were busy at the mine, the Cherry Relief Committee dispensed food and clothing. The list of people who donated to the *Chicago Daily Tribune*'s relief fund grew longer every day. On Thursday, Frank Moy, a Chinese immigrant, gave $50 donated by Chicago's Chinese Merchants Association. He enclosed a note that stated: "My countrymen in Chicago sympathize with the poor women and children of Cherry, and I wish we were able to send 100 times the amount. The American people have always responded to an appeal for help from China." The Cook County [Illinois] Teachers' Association donated $41.25. A woman who empathized with the women of Cherry and wished only to be acknowledged as "a widow" donated $1.00. By Thursday, the *Tribune*'s fund totaled more than $12,000.

Labor unions supported the victims' families. The national Painters' Union donated $1,000 to the United Mine Workers' Cherry relief fund.

The St. Paul Coal Company taxed the wage of each of its employees twenty-five cents. This generated $12,000 to $15,000 that was earmarked for the victims' families according to need.

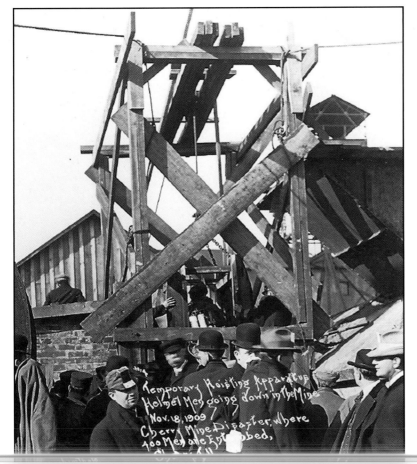

Temporary Hoisting Apparatus Holmes Men going down in the Mine Nov. 18, 1909 Cherry Mine Disaster where 400 Men are Entombed, Princeton, Ill.

After mine inspectors decided on a rescue plan, carpenters built a framework above the air shaft. A bucket suspended in it was used to raise and lower men into the mine. In this photo, one of the rescuers is inside the bucket, ready to descend into the air shaft. Oxygen tanks are strapped to his back.

Everyone who donated did so because they cared. It didn't matter if those in need originally came from another country. It didn't matter if some of them couldn't speak English. All that mattered was helping people in need.

Donations of food, blankets, and warm clothing eased some of the worries that weighed on the families of the dead and missing miners, but donations didn't ease their sorrow. Miner Celestino Menietti and his brother had escaped from the third vein. As he walked the streets of Cherry that night, he was reminded that many men hadn't. He heard people crying inside every home that he passed.

FRIDAY, NOVEMBER 19: DAY 7
UNDERGROUND

In their three-hundred-foot-long underground prison, the men in Walter Waite and George Eddy's group were no longer sure what day it was. Some thought it was Saturday. While he waited for his turn to drink, Antenore Quartaroli spoke with Thomas White, who said that he thought it was Friday. White told Quartaroli that in England and Scotland, the country where he was born, Friday was a day that brought good luck. That he hoped it would bring new hope and give him the strength to fight until death. Quartaroli told White that Italians considered Friday a day of misfortune. If he died, he would rather it not be on a Friday. White urged him not to give up hope. It was hard. Even though he and White had waited by their water hole for a long time, it remained dry. It took all of Quartaroli's strength to stagger into a far area of the tunnel where he found a small hole with scarcely a mouthful of water. He told the others about the hole when he managed to rejoin them. But it was not a promising source of water for the group.

One time, Walter Waite picked open a small hole in one of the barricades. He felt a faint air current. The fan was running! Waite bolstered his comrades' hopes with the news.

"We are better off than those on top; for we know we are alive, and they don't know it," he urged. "Don't give up. We are going to give those people up there the very biggest surprise they ever had, yet."

But their fight to survive was getting harder. At times, George Eddy was delirious. Ruggeri Buonfiglio kept talking about food. Several times, Walter Waite told everyone about ten bananas he had purchased from an Italian street vendor several years before. He had eaten every one. The men pleaded for Buonfiglio and Waite to stop. No one could bear hearing about food. Sleep offered little comfort: dreams teased of safety, while nightmares promised death.

Waite and Giacomo Pigati worried that fresh air would never reach their enclosure. Pigati knew they couldn't last much longer without more water. He suggested a plan. A search party could break through one of the walls and hunt for water. If they didn't find water and black damp overcame them . . . well . . . that would be their end.

William Clelland spoke up. He suggested that they not break down the wall completely, but that someone should go out and test the strength of the black damp. The group agreed. They broke a hole just big enough for a man to squeeze through, and Clelland went out.

The group waited for what seemed an eternity.

Then Clelland returned with bad news. "I am sorry to tell you that the black damp is still strong, and I don't believe that any of us can resist the black damp to where there is water."

Despair overwhelmed them. As he had before, Walter Waite calmed them and offered hope. He said they would wait and try again the next day. In the meantime, the man whose strength remained strongest would take a lunch pail and search all of the water holes in the passageways within their enclosure. He would collect the water in the lunch pail and bring it back for everyone to share.

The Pigati brothers volunteered. Feeling their way around the chamber, they searched all of the water holes that had been dug throughout the main chamber's area. After a long time, they returned with an empty pail.

The brothers rested to regain strength, then set out again to search side passageways.

As the time dragged, Antenore Quartaroli prayed for the brothers' return. He hadn't had any water for almost twenty-four hours. His mouth felt like "a fiery furnace."

But the brothers did not return.

ON THE SURFACE
FRIDAY

Friday morning, rescuers and miners investigated more of the second vein. Just being inside the mine was horrific. The stench of the mules' decaying bodies was so bad that men had to cover their mouths and noses. They gingerly made their way along some passages, shoring up timbers as they went. Cave-ins and dead mules blocked the way into other passageways. The miners started the huge job of shoveling fallen rock into pit cars for removal. They pushed the pit cars by hand. All the mules were dead. Carpenters began building a special car to remove the mules' remains from the passageways. Removing human remains that lay beyond cave-ins wouldn't be possible until the roadways were clear. Rescue party members estimated they had seen eighty bodies.

Four bodies were brought to the surface on Friday. While the rescue party carried more bodies toward the shaft, the ceiling cracked

It was a sad, somber time when workers carried a victim's body away from the shaft to the morgue.

loudly. They ran for their lives. Moments after reaching safety, several tons of earth crashed down behind them and buried the bodies they had been carrying.

On the surface, the four recovered bodies lay side by side on a length of white canvas. Women walked past them, searching for a missing husband or brother. Malinda Dobbins, Charlie and Walter Waite's sister, was among them. Suddenly, Malinda gasped. At first, she had not recognized the charred body. But when she looked closely at his shirt, she noticed a peculiar button. She knew that button: she had sewn it on her brother Charlie's shirt the week before! She screamed and fainted. Soldiers from the Illinois National Guard carried her to an ambulance, which brought her home, where a nurse remained with her for the night. She was in a state of shock: Charlie was dead. Anna Waite was told that her husband Charlie's body had been recovered. Walter Waite was still in the mine.

There was news that some areas not far from the hoisting shaft still smoldered. On Friday afternoon, a company of Chicago firefighters descended in the hoisting shaft cage. They directed all miners, carpenters, and rescue party members to leave the mine. Dragging very long hoses, the firefighters blasted the roadways with streams of water. They moved into the mule stable and the passageway to the air shaft, and continued as far as their hoses could reach. By late afternoon, they believed the fire was completely extinguished. The fire chief reported that men could resume clearing rubble and removing bodies the next morning.

A large number of miners were missing. Each time a victim's remains reached the morgue, people formed a line outside, waiting to enter and search for a missing relative or friend.

Men also set up a new morgue—a very large tent loaned by a Civil War veterans group—just beyond the end of the tipple. It had quickly become clear that the shed used to shelter the remains of the twelve dead rescuers was too small. Reports given to the coroner about the condition of the bodies in the mine led him to the decision that for health reasons, all bodies recovered from that point on had to be treated with disinfectants before being placed in the morgue.

By the end of the day Friday, a mine inspector stated, "After a week's work we have at last succeeded in extinguishing the fire. The bringing out of the bodies necessarily will be slow. In fact, I do not expect it to be completed before Sunday or Monday."

The previous night, the president of the Illinois Mining Commission and the chief inspector in charge of the rescue work had grimly announced to reporters, "There is not the slightest hope that any are living, but the bereaved [families] on top are deserving of the search."

Although the inspectors had given up hope, the miners' families had not.

It wasn't long before the shed used as a temporary morgue was too small to hold recovered bodies. A white canvas tent replaced it as the morgue.

CHAPTER 12
MAD CHEERING

SATURDAY, NOVEMBER 20: DAY 8
UNDERGROUND

Antenore Quartaroli was worried about the Pigatis. They'd been gone
for hours. George Eddy's throat was so dry, he could not speak any
louder than a whisper. Daniel Holofzak wheezed with every breath.
Leopold Dumont was close to death. Without water, everyone would
soon die. In desperation, Walter Waite and William Clelland also left
on a water search.

Someone said, "It's time to get up courage and make another
attempt [to get to the hoisting shaft]." Quartaroli, Francesco Zanarini,
and Ruggeri Buonfiglio mustered every bit of energy. Still within

the barricaded chamber, they moved along the tunnel in a direction toward the roadways that went to the hoisting shaft.

After walking what seemed a long way, the three men encountered Walter Waite. Waite had found some water—only about a cupful. He had saved it to share with everyone.

While the group rested to regain strength, they heard noises. Tired, dragging footsteps. It was the Pigati brothers! They had searched for water all night. But all they collected was a ragful of dirty water, enough only to dampen their lips.

"I don't expect to live 5 minutes more. I'll break [the] wall and try to walk . . . I don't care if I die from black damp. Rather than suffer this way, I prefer death," said Giacomo Pigati.

Waite said he thought there would be water in the tunnels south of their location. He suggested that several of the strongest men take some lunch pails, leave the barricaded chamber, and seek that water. They could return with water for the others.

Courageously, Frank Waite, a young man who had emigrated from England a few months earlier and may have been related to Walter, volunteered. He and Walter broke a hole in one of the barricades. Walter sensed moving air. The mine was unsealed! But that had happened before. It didn't raise their hopes much.

Frank squeezed through the hole and walked south, as Walter had suggested. He was gone more than an hour. He returned, dizzy from black damp, but carrying enough water for each man to wet his mouth.

Knowing they could not last much longer, Walter Waite again

asked for courage. "I ask those of you who feel strong enough to attempt the last chance."

Giacomo and Salvatore Pigati said they would go. Francesco Zanarini agreed to go with them.

George Eddy was too weak. He whispered to Walter Waite, "I will stay here and if I am not rescued here they will find my body where I now lay." He thought he would never see daylight again.

Thomas White's lips and tongue were so swollen from lack of water that he couldn't speak. He was so weak that he couldn't raise his hand to volunteer.

One man, George Stimez, had slightly more strength remaining than the others. He finally agreed he would go too, so each man had a partner.

Walter Waite gave the cupful of water that he had saved to Giacomo Pigati to use on their walk. Walter told them that when they reached a certain passageway, they should whistle twice if the air was good and whistle once if it wasn't.

Antenore Quartaroli shook hands with his three friends for what he believed was the last time and the four men left.

Everyone's ears strained for the sound of a whistle. But they heard nothing.

An hour passed.

Still nothing.

Had their companions forgotten to signal?

Or had black damp killed them?

Saturday morning, miners resumed Friday's rescue work. Most of the workers were Cherry Mine employees; some were from other Illinois mines. Robert Clelland, William's brother, worked in a mine seventy miles away. He'd been rescued after a mine accident earlier that year and knew rescue teams always needed men. When he heard his brother was missing, he volunteered to help in any way he could, even if it meant recovering bodies.

Going to the morgue to view remains was a heartbreaking task for relatives and friends.

David Powell, the superintendent in the mine where Robert Clelland worked, also volunteered. In Cherry, he teamed with Father James Haney, a priest from a church in Mendota, Illinois, to lead a six-man rescue party.

With picks and shovels, men attacked piles of fallen rock in the second vein. Rescuers hadn't forgotten the men in the third vein. But they felt that survivors in the second vein, being closer to the fire, were more threatened. Some workers had the grim task of hauling dead mules to the hoisting cage. Others carried human remains. By early afternoon, about fifty bodies had been placed in lines in a nearby field. After treating the bodies with disinfectants, men carried the remains to the white tent that served as the morgue.

The remains were not easily recognized due to the fire and the time elapsed. Men hired to help the coroner searched each body for items that would aid in identification. They particularly looked for the metal tag that a miner hung from his loaded pit car. When they found one, they checked the tag's number against the company books, which listed the name of the man who had been given that tag. Personal items—such as a pocket watch, a pipe, a wallet, or a knife—also helped identify victims.

Women, many holding a child's hand or carrying an infant, hurried to the large tent. Men told them to go home, believing that the women wouldn't be able to handle seeing the remains. But the women refused to leave. These were their husbands, brothers, and fathers. It was their right to identify them and see to their burial. Viewing the bodies was a grisly task. Some people fainted. One woman could

Sadly, the only way some remains could be identified was by the items they carried in their pockets or by distinctive clothing.

Cherry, Ill. Nov 13, 09
a portion of 31 victems
found $190.00 on body
back ground table, by F.J.K., Peru, Ill.
a/or 11, 10.

#26

only recognize her husband's body because he had been missing a finger. The coroner's men placed identified victims in pine coffins and sent them to the victims' homes, where the family grieved until the funeral and burial.

For seven days, Lena Waite, Walter's wife, had come to the mine shaft seeking news of her missing husband. That morning, Lena spent hours viewing remains in the morgue. At noon, she was emotionally and physically exhausted. She walked home and prepared food for her four children. Afterward, she was so tired that she lay down for a short rest.

At times, George Eddy's wife, Elizabeth, and her three daughters had joined their neighbor Lena Waite near the mine as they sought news about George.

Celina Howard and Mamie Robinson also spent hours at the morgue. They found neither Sam nor Alfred. Hoping that her sons were still alive, Celina Howard left the morgue with a new worry: Were rescue efforts taking so long that her boys would starve to death?

WORRIED AND WAITING
UNDERGROUND, SATURDAY

Meanwhile, Walter Waite, Clelland, Quartaroli, and Frank Waite discussed what to do. The four searchers hadn't whistled. They hadn't returned. If black damp had killed them, it would kill another search party too. But doing nothing meant certain death. Clelland, Frank Waite, and Quartaroli decided to go, but would take a different passageway from the one their companions had taken. It would eventually connect with tunnels that went south toward water.

As they left, Walter Waite said, "Brothers[,] have courage, see that you do the best you can[.] I wish you good luck." Quartaroli repeated Walter's words to himself again and again as he, Clelland, and Frank Waite struggled along the passageway.

Shortly after leaving, Quartaroli fell. He hit his head and was knocked unconscious for a moment. Frank Waite and Clelland waited with him until he recovered. They moved forward at a snail's pace—only four or five steps at a time—because the air was not good. Breathing was difficult. They crawled over piles of rock and squeezed around fallen timbers. Clelland felt the face of his watch. They'd been traveling for more than half an hour. Every few minutes they called out to the Pigatis but received no response. Quartaroli feared they were dead. He thought he was going to die too.

Finally, they reached a wider roadway. Quartaroli froze. He heard a noise. He called out. He was overjoyed when Francesco Zanarini answered. He heard more voices—the Pigatis! Quartaroli felt as though his heart received a jolt of energy. He, Frank Waite, and Clelland followed the voices and reunited with the others.

The seven men walked on. Once, they turned the wrong way. But they soon found the passageway that led south, toward water. Traces of black damp robbed their energy and slowed their progress. It took them half an hour to go only a little more than thirty feet, the distance between the passageways that led to different workstations.

They gagged and covered their noses when they passed dead

mules. But they were encouraged: even though the air smelled terrible, it was fresher air, not black damp. Breathing was easier. As loudly as they could, they whistled twice to their companions who awaited their signal back in the barricaded area.

Giacomo Pigati felt his way along a pit car track. He bumped into a loaded pit car. He kept his hand on the car until he discovered that its chain was still hitched to a mule. The mule would have been heading toward the hoisting shaft. Now they knew for certain that they were going in the correct direction!

They pushed open a pair of ventilation doors. Then Quartaroli knew exactly where he was and that a barrel of water was kept close by. But when he reached it, the barrel had been tipped over and was dry. He asked Giacomo Pigati if he still had any water. Pigati handed him a wet cloth so he could dampen his lips. That was all they had.

By then, five more men had left the barricaded chamber and joined them. Too weak to walk, Walter Waite, George Eddy, Thomas White, John Lorimer, and Ruggeri Buonfiglio had remained behind the barricade.

The twelve men continued on, their spirits buoyed by the belief they would find life-saving water soon.

Their good spirits crashed when they saw a dim, flickering light. Fire!

They had gotten within five hundred feet of the hoisting shaft, only to be beaten by flames. Everyone groaned with despair.

The light disappeared. The men shouted and whistled but received no answer.

The dim, yellow light reappeared, flickered, and again disappeared.

Determined to reach the hoisting shaft, the men walked on. Just before they reached the main roadway to the hoisting shaft, they smelled really fresh air. It came from the direction of the air shaft. They decided to go there instead.

When they turned a corner to approach the air shaft, Quartaroli quickly closed his eyes. Glimmering yellow lights hurt them. He opened his eyelids a crack. The lights were still there! They were sunshine lamps hooked on the caps of men near the air shaft! Quartaroli cried out with joy. The first face he saw belonged to one of his brothers-in-law, his wife's brother! As they tightly hugged each other, Antenore asked again and again about Erminia and his son. He was frantic to know they were all right. His brother-in-law assured him they were.

At two o'clock, David Powell's six-man rescue party had descended into the mine. Within minutes, they heard shouts that survivors had been found. They ran to the thirst-starved men and offered them water, only a mouthful at a time. William Clelland asked what day it was. It surprised him to learn it was Saturday. Like many of the survivors, he had thought it was Sunday. But that no longer mattered: they had been rescued! Clelland told Powell where the men barricaded deeper in the mine were. Hurry to them, he urged, they are very weak.

When Antenore Quartaroli reached the hoisting shaft, another brother-in-law ran up and hugged him. He said Quartaroli's brother had come from Iowa and was waiting at home with Erminia and the baby. All Quartaroli wanted was to see his family!

Great excitement and hope filled everyone when a worker shouted that men had been found alive!

"They are alive"
THE FIRST LIVING RESCUED
2 30 P.M. Sat. 20-09
N CHURCHILL Photo
PERU, ILL

A member of Powell's rescue party shouted up the hoisting shaft that survivors had been found. The worker at the top yelled the news to everyone within earshot. The sheriff, who was near the shaft, shouted the news to the clerk in the mine office. He ordered the clerk to send for the doctors and nurses.

People shouted the news throughout Cherry's streets. Women dropped their work. They picked up babies, grabbed hold of toddlers' hands, and ran toward the mine. Storekeepers hustled shoppers out to the sidewalk, locked the store doors, and ran to the mine. In less than half an hour, the crowd around the hoisting shaft—newspaper reporters, photographers, family members, miners—had doubled, then tripled in size. Fighting for a glimpse of the survivors, people shoved aside the soldiers who surrounded the hoisting shaft. No one knew how many had been rescued. Reports ranged from just a few to a hundred. Families waited in agony.

BARRICADE DOWN

Following Clelland's directions, David Powell's rescue team weaved around obstacles and along passageways until a pile of debris blocked their way. The party yelled, then stood quiet. A moment passed. Then they heard faint pounding. The rescuers tore into the barricade, tossing rocks aside and chopping at timbers with picks and axes. Finally, loose dirt tumbled from the top of the barricade.

Father Haney and Powell called into the hole. *Is anyone there? Is anyone alive?*

Faint voices from the darkness answered: *Yes. Do you have food?*

"Be patient as you can," Father Haney replied. "We will get you out in a minute and give you all the lunch you can eat." He assured the survivors that the hoisting cage was ready and waiting for them.

With renewed haste, the rescue party pulled more debris from the barricade and opened a large gap. They handed a lamp through the hole.

Seeing the survivors thrilled Haney. "With a shout we jumped over and met them, throwing our arms around their necks and almost lifting them from their feet. . . . Their joy was inexpressible. They pounded us on our backs and continued to laugh and cry aloud until the whole place reverberated with the cheering."

The light and the sound of loud voices roused Thomas White from a half stupor. A rescuer gave him a swallow of water. White begged for more. Not right away, his rescuer said. You'll throw it up. He told White there was plenty more water, and he could have another mouthful in a few minutes.

George Eddy thought he was imagining the rescuers. When he realized the rescue party was truly there, he became so dizzy with relief he couldn't stand.

Father Haney was concerned to learn that one of the men was very near death. He moved farther into the chamber and knelt beside Leopold Dumont, the Belgian. Dumont weakly told the priest he was afraid he would "never get up alive." Father Haney prayed with Dumont and blessed him. Dumont died shortly afterward. He had no family in Cherry.

David Powell told the survivors that the rescue party would carry them to the hoisting shaft. But regular sips of water had restored some of the men. They insisted on walking. Thomas White made it to the bottom of the shaft and then collapsed. George Eddy needed supportive arms all the way. Daniel Holofzak barely clung to life. Rescuers carried him, unconscious, to the shaft.

Dr. Howe had already reached the second vein and had treated the first men found. He injected them with medicine that stimulated their hearts. He gave them oxygen and wrapped a blanket around those who shivered in the cold, fresh air. Howe treated Powell's group of survivors as they arrived near the shaft. He kept all the survivors in the mine until everyone was stabilized. Finally, he decided they were in good enough shape to go up.

Howe draped a piece of canvas over each survivor's head as they entered the cage. After so many days in total darkness, their eyes needed protection from the day's remaining sunlight. Many of the survivors told Howe they wanted to go straight home. He refused to allow that. Ten doctors and as many nurses waited in three railroad cars set up as hospitals. No survivor was going anywhere until he was further examined, treated, and given light foods, such as warm milk and broth. To the survivors' dismay, no wives or children could visit them until the doctors okayed it.

Francesco Zanarini was the first one up. Antenore Quartaroli was next. After that, the survivors came up in groups of two or three.

Thomas White, a blanket wrapped around his shoulders and canvas draped over his head, felt cold air when the cage reached the surface. As he left the cage, he heard the "mad cheering of a tremendous crowd that had gathered at the top of the shaft. . . . I could not see them, but the noise they made showed me that their number was large." He entered a hospital car but was determined that he would be at home with his pregnant wife, Margaret, and their two young children before nightfall.

Walter Waite still remained below. Rescuers standing around him said they believed many men, maybe one hundred, were alive in the mine. Waite threw off his blanket and struggled to his feet.

"I'm not going out of this mine until I get the others," he declared.

Father Haney held Waite. Told him that he needed fresh air and food or he might die. Waite struggled free. Rescuers finally forced Waite into the cage, promising that after he had some rest and food, they might let him join a rescue party.

In town, a short time earlier, Walter's wife, Lena, had been resting in bed. She heard voices outside, and someone knocked on her front door. When she answered, the person on her porch said, "They say living men are coming out of the mine, and they say Mr. Waite is with them!" Lena dressed faster than she'd ever thought possible and ran to the mine. The news was true! Walter was in one of the hospital cars. She stood beside the railroad car and wept with relief.

Shortly afterward, seventeen-year-old Florence Eddy had been stunned when her uncle rushed to her house, yelling, "They have found living men—men are alive!" Florence believed "hope gave wings to my feet" as she ran to the mine. Florence's hopes rose and fell as the cage lifted men up. But she couldn't see them. And then, as she stood at the rope cordoning the hoisting shaft, she heard the news that her father was alive. He wouldn't be coming up right away, though, because he was very weak. But that was all right. "It was a relief to know that he was alive, so [my family] could wait for him with lighter hearts," Florence recalled.

Robert Clelland, William Clelland's brother, was among the volunteers who brought survivors to the surface. After he helped a survivor off the cage and turned back for another trip down, a friend tapped him on the shoulder.

"Bob, don't you know that Will is up?" the man asked.

Clelland was stunned. Could it be true?

"Yes, alive. He's up alive. Why, Bob, you brought him up yourself, wrapped in blankets," his friend said.

Robert couldn't believe he'd missed seeing William. But no one had said who was covered up. And William, with his head draped, wouldn't have seen him. After finding out that William was doing well, Robert ran to tell William's wife the fantastic news.

Finally, all the survivors lay in the hospital cars. William McClelland and others raised the car windows, stuck their heads out, and waved. They searched the crowd for their families. Antenore Quartaroli spotted Erminia, his brother, and "all those who were dear to my heart." Erminia begged the soldiers to open the railroad car door so she could care for her husband, but they refused. Later,

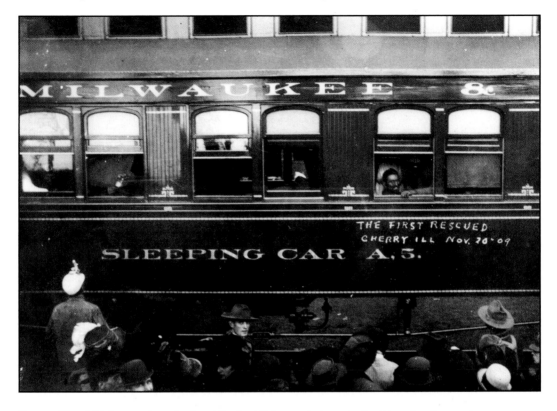

Some of the eight-day survivors look out the hospital car windows, trying to see family members.

though, a sympathetic guard let her in. "It was a joy to embrace, as neither of us thought we would be together again," Quartaroli recalled.

It wasn't long before the wives of George Eddy, William Clelland, Giacomo Pigati, William Waite, and other survivors were allowed in too. At 7:00 p.m., doctors released some of the survivors. But Florence Eddy still waited impatiently outside the hospital car. "It was 9 o'clock that evening before my two sisters and I were given permission to visit my father."

William Clelland
was relieved
and happy to be
reunited with his
family. But he
was angry that so
many men had died
needlessly.

Peter Donna, who had escaped from the third vein with his father a week earlier, sat outside the hospital cars in a horse-drawn carriage. He was offering the survivors a ride home. Thomas White gladly accepted.

Quartaroli kindly refused the offer of a ride. He said that his wife and baby were at his brother-in-law's house only a short distance away. Walking would be quicker. A few minutes later, he held his baby son. He wanted to never let him go again.

Daniel Holofzak also walked home. He'd recovered some strength and refused to be confined inside a carriage.

Finding survivors energized the crowd. The rumor that many more men could be alive renewed Celina Howard, Mamie Robinson, and Mary and Albert Buckel's hopes. Jessie Love had not found her husband, John, or his brothers in the morgue. Maybe there was hope for them too.

Earlier that day, Jessie had received a letter from her brother Robert Deans. He was in a hotel in Chicago. In the short letter, he told her that he would come back to Cherry; he just had to be away for now. He cautioned her not to tell anyone where he was. Jessie knew Robert had no money. She was certain someone from the coal company had given him money and told him to stay away.

CHAPTER 13
MORE FLAMES

On Saturday, several rescuers working in the second vein thought they heard distant voices and pounding beyond one of the cave-ins. The news galvanized rescue and recovery parties Sunday morning. Many miners wanted to quickly clear the blocked passage. The inspectors disagreed. Certain that the miners' route risked more cave-ins, they suggested another path. They did not want to sacrifice rescuers.

Diggers worked shifts round-the-clock. A Lithuanian miner remained in the tunnels thirty-six hours before collapsing with exhaustion. He was carried from the mine. Speaking in his native language, he told union officials that coal company bosses wouldn't let him come up. A volunteer miner from another town worked even longer. When the coroner heard about it, he gave the man money to pay for a room in Cherry's hotel and told him to get a good night's sleep.

Mine inspectors forbade a group of rescuers from entering one tunnel. Angrily, the rescuers threw down their tools and refused to work elsewhere. They resumed work in another area only after learning that the level of black damp in the tunnel they had planned to enter was dangerously high.

Avoiding black damp was a constant battle. In fact, one rescuer, a mining engineer named John Collins, came within minutes of death when he encountered the toxic gas. Anxious to reach survivors, Collins crawled up a pile of loose earth and rock that blocked a passageway. He crept forward along the top of the pile. Suddenly, the flame of his sunshine lamp went out. Black damp had extinguished it! Collins lost consciousness. He would have died if another rescuer hadn't noticed, grabbed Collins's feet, and dragged him to safety. When Collins regained consciousness, he reported grim news. Dead mules and the bodies of dead miners covered the tunnel floor beyond the cave-in. Entering that passageway before the air near the debris pile cleared meant certain death. Collins thought that the air at the far end of the tunnel, away from the barricade, might still be clear. That part of the tunnel, in his opinion, might be the rescuers' last best hope for finding survivors in the second vein.

Inspectors frequently visited the fan house and checked that the fan was blowing as much fresh air into the mine as was safe. It was the only way to stop black damp from accumulating. Even with the fan operating, rescuers needed helmets and oxygen tanks in some tunnels.

Although tons of water had flooded the mine, embers still smoldered deep within debris piles and crevices. A small fire flared up about fifty feet from the hoisting shaft. Chicago firefighters quickly extinguished it. All day and into the night, they battled small fiery outbreaks.

Forty-nine bodies were removed from the mine on Sunday. Rescuers saw dozens more bodies but had not yet removed them. Their focus was on finding survivors. They removed only those remains that blocked their path toward tunnels where men might still be alive. As the hours passed, the hope of finding more survivors dimmed.

But they could not completely ignore the bodies. Safety inspectors feared they would become a health hazard as they decayed. Workers spread disinfectants on the remains to slow decay and prevent contamination.

Rescuers demanded that the inspectors let them go to the third vein. No one had explored it yet, and they believed survivors might be there. Water that flowed down from the flooded second vein might be keeping them alive. The inspectors refused. They felt that any remaining survivors in the second vein were within hours, if not minutes, of death. Like Walter Waite's group, they would have little or no water to sustain them. They had to be found first. The inspectors promised that rescuers could explore the third vein the next day.

Telephone calls, telegrams, and newspaper articles spread news of Saturday's miraculous rescue across the United States. Again, a steady stream of automobiles, carriages, and wagons rolled into Cherry. More than twenty thousand gawkers arrived. The sheriff called in all his deputies for crowd control.

From the moment news spread that there was a fire in the mine, a crowd of varying size kept a days-long vigil near the shafts.

Cherry mine disaster. More than 300 Miners lost their lives bombed in this Furnace. Nov 13 1909. Cherry, Ill 16714. Photo by C. U. Williams Bloomington, Ill

Mourners stood outside both churches and watched clergymen conduct funeral services. (Health inspectors had requested that all funerals be held outdoors as a precaution against health hazards.) Gawkers lined Main Street as a funeral procession carried eighteen caskets to the cemetery at the south end of town. They watched wagons loaded with more caskets leave Cherry for cemeteries in nearby towns.

In town, nurses distributed medicines and brought food from the relief warehouse to miners' families three times daily. The *Chicago Daily Tribune*, whose relief fund had collected almost $25,000, sent more money to Cherry. People contributed as their life circumstances permitted. No amount was too small. Five-year-old Ladon Gallie, who lived in Chicago, wanted to help the children. She donated 239 pennies—all the money she had in her bank—to the relief efforts. Then she organized a relief fund among her friends.

Red Cross director Ernest Bicknell paid off the mortgages on the homes of miners' widows with some of the relief funds. This prevented them from becoming homeless.

At the morgue, Celina Howard viewed the remains brought up that day, but had not found Sam or Alfred. A woman near her sobbed, "I know they are alive. My man is down there. God will save him."

Jessie Love already knew that one of her brothers-in-law was dead; his body had been recovered. But her husband, John, and his other two brothers were still in the mine. She knew their chances were slim.

This widow, who has been tentatively identified as Alice Mills, placed her husband's photo inside a brooch as a sign of remembrance. Her husband, Arthur, died in the disaster. They had two young children.

One woman in the crowd said, "The men they brought up could not have lived more than a few hours longer. If they don't come up today they'll come up dead."

Sunday night, rescuers had cleared a large cave-in. Monday morning, rescue parties traveled deep into the southeastern tunnel beyond it. Sadly, they didn't find survivors. Instead, they found twenty-nine victims. They were behind a set of the ventilation doors used to control the direction of air currents. The bodies lay huddled near three makeshift fans that had been cobbled together from pieces of wood, wire, pick handles, and other items. Sam and Alfred Howard's bodies were among the dead men near the fans. They had done their best to circulate air and ward off black damp. Sadly, their efforts were in vain. Rescuers found more victims in other tunnels.

Throughout the day, rescue crews sent more bodies to the morgue. Since recovery efforts had begun, the crews had brought up a total of one hundred bodies. The coroner, his assistants, and many women stayed in the morgue until after 9:00 p.m. trying to identify bodies. They found a number of goodbye notes tucked into pockets.

Celina Howard's search for Sam and Alfred ended when one of the coroner's helpers placed Sam's diary in her hands. She clasped the diary. Together, she and Mamie Robinson identified Sam's and Alfred's bodies. Workers fastened lids on the brothers' coffins, and a wagon took their remains to the Howards' home.

At his home, Walter Waite held out little hope for any men still below.

"I believe they are all dead," he told a reporter. "I hope I am wrong, but there is no use holding out false hopes. . . . I know the mine like a book. . . . I believe none of the entombed men is now alive."

Again, men worked through the night. Inspectors tested the air quality and temperature in the third vein. They found it clear and cool and approved exploration.

The only way down to the third vein from the hoisting shaft was via the small emergency cage that rested in the third vein, at the bottom of the shaft. One end of a long rope was always tied to the emergency cage. The other end was in the second vein. Men attached this end of the rope to the bottom of the large hoisting cage. The engineer raised the large hoisting cage until the small emergency cage neared the second vein. He didn't raise it all the way to the second vein because the timbers weren't safe. Three volunteers slid down the rope and landed on top of the emergency cage. They rode on top of the cage as the engineer lowered it to the third vein.

Water, nearly waist-deep, filled the tunnel. The three men waded along the slanting roadway until they reached higher ground. They hoped survivors would be there. Unfortunately, all they found were a few lunch pails and a pile of rocks and broken timbers.

The three explorers returned to the cage. Partway up, the cage got stuck. Cold air from the surface blew down on the sopping wet men. Chilled to the bone, they abandoned the cage and climbed one hundred feet up the shaft's timber frame. Just below the second vein, firefighters hung a makeshift sling down to them. One by one, they hauled the men up. The three reported that the third vein should be

Watches were often among the personal items found on the victims' bodies that were sometimes the only way to identify remains.

fully explored the next day, and that pumping water out of the third vein would be a good idea.

Meanwhile, fire flared again near the hoisting shaft. Safety inspectors ordered all rescuers out of the mine.

TUESDAY, NOVEMBER 23

Firefighters spent Monday night and most of Tuesday drenching the hoisting shaft's timber supports. The bodies of fourteen more victims had been recovered, but by midmorning, inspectors again ordered recovery crews out of the mine. The amount of another gas, carbon dioxide, had risen to an alarming level. Too much carbon dioxide would be as fatal to rescuers as black damp.

On Tuesday morning, Steele Street residents received sad news: their neighbor Daniel Holofzak had died. Being exposed to poor air, starvation, and lack of water for a week was more than his already frail health could bear. Grief replaced the happiness his wife and their eight children had felt just two days earlier.

Sam and Alfred Howard's funeral was held Tuesday afternoon. Afterward, a newspaper reporter spoke with Mamie Robinson. She told him, "Sam and I were going to be married on Christmas day. He was brave and good and we are proud of him." That morning, the postmaster had given Mamie the ring that Sam had left with him.

Gradually, the gawkers left Cherry. The governor ordered one

When the situation in Cherry had settled down, the governor ordered one of the National Guard companies to return home.

of the National Guard companies to return to its home base. Nurses continued treating people, and the Cherry Relief Committee distributed more food and clothes. The *Chicago Daily Tribune*'s relief fund had passed $30,000. Added to the funds donated directly to the Red Cross, the relief fund totaled almost $60,000.

WEDNESDAY, NOVEMBER 24

On Wednesday, as soon as the inspectors allowed, rescuers descended to the third vein. They went farther along the slanted passageway than the volunteers had the previous night and waded through four tunnels. Sadly, they found a large number of bodies in a dry area about five hundred feet from the hoisting shaft. Like Walter Waite's group, the victims had tried to avoid black damp by closing off their tunnel with a large canvas curtain. Like Sam Howard's companions, they'd made a makeshift fan from wooden boxes. But neither preventive action had worked. Notes found with their bodies indicated that the men had been dead for about a week.

Recovering bodies from the third vein would not be possible until the water was pumped out. The inspectors made arrangements to install a pump and pipeline so recovery efforts could resume as soon as possible.

As night fell, more fires broke out in places near the hoisting shaft. Firefighters stoutheartedly battled the flames but couldn't extinguish them. And the odor of the smoke had changed. It no longer smelled like burning timber; it smelled like burning coal. Fire had spread into the coal still buried within the second vein's thick pillars.

In the middle of the night, the commissioner in charge of the rescue efforts called an emergency conference with the state inspectors. The numerous blazes burning inside the pillars were beyond the firefighters' control. The temperature in the mine had risen to 107°F

(42° C). At that point, everyone knew the only way to extinguish the fire was by starving it of oxygen. They had to reseal both shafts.

Although no more survivors had been found after Saturday, people clung to the slimmest hope that loved ones in the third vein might be alive. Many family members still clustered around the hoisting shaft. Dismayed moans filled the air when they saw workers permanently seal the hoisting and air shafts with concrete slabs and steel beams. All hopes of finding more survivors ended.

The workers finished their task shortly before dawn on Thursday, November 25.

It was Thanksgiving Day.

Sam Howard and his companions built fans similar to this one as they struggled to survive. This fan was found in April 1910, probably in the third vein.

CHAPTER 14

WIDOWS, ORPHANS, BLAME

When inspectors permanently sealed the hoisting shaft, they left a small hole in the concrete cap. They lowered a thermometer through the opening and took the shaft's temperature daily. The first week of December, it was still 113°F (45°C). They also tested the air quality, which was poor.

On February 1, 1910, almost three months after the disaster, inspectors announced that it was safe to reopen the mine. Workers broke open the concrete caps and started the fan. The fire seemed to be almost out, but the ceilings and walls were in dangerous condition. For days, experts debated how to safely clear the many cave-ins. At first, only one mule was lowered into the mine to haul debris-loaded pit cars. More followed as cleared space opened up.

No 30
Cherry Mine
Disaster
Removing seal from shaft Feb 1 1910

In February 1910, mine inspectors finally felt it was safe to reopen the mine and resume recovering the victims' remains.

Recovery teams explored the second and third veins. They pumped water out of the mine and treated it with chemicals that killed harmful bacteria. Finally, they began the search for bodies.

Throughout February, March, and April, family members returned to the morgue as men carried more than one hundred victims from the mine. By then, identification of the bodies was, in some cases, impossible.

February through April 1910 were sad months for many Cherry residents as church services, funeral processions, and the burial of victims continued.

Italian Funeral Passing through Cherry, Mich. 6. With Victims of Mine Disaster.

Dunham Photo
Princeton, Ill.

Funeral processions again rolled along Main Street and to the cemetery, where the victims were buried near their former colleagues. Two hundred fifty-nine men died in the fire. Almost every family in town lost someone.

Small fires still smoldered in the mine well into May. The remains of the final victim to be found were lifted from the mine in July.

LONG-TERM HELP

Months after the fire, Red Cross director Ernest Bicknell wrote, "Any great disaster instantly arouses the generosity of the American people." Response to the disaster proved it. In total, donations from the general public, the Red Cross, the United Mine Workers, the State of Illinois, and coal operators raised over $400,000. Nurses supplied by the St. Paul Coal Company and representatives from the Red Cross remained in Cherry all winter during 1909–1910. That season, the coal company did not collect rent from miners' families who lived in company-owned houses. Without this assistance, miners' families wouldn't have received food, clothing, medical attention, or shelter. A widow might have been forced to place one or more of her children in an orphanage if the family's situation had become dire. In June 1910, the original Cherry Relief Committee, designed for emergency service, disbanded. A new group called the

The Cherry Relief Commission made sure that children received nourishing meals.

Cherry Relief Commission assumed responsibility for permanent relief. The commission believed that the "holding of families intact, the education of the children, [and] the improvement of home life" were essential.

Temporary help had been important, but the commission's permanent help was crucial. In the early 1900s, most women did not work outside the home. After the fire, 390 children lived in families without a main wage earner. Some widows earned money by renting a room to one or more boarders. But most had no source of income. This was a big problem that the Cherry Relief Commission intended to solve with the $85,837.96 left in its relief fund.

On June 20, 1910, commission members contacted a reliable bank in Chicago and set up a special account. They created two plans for giving money to victims' families.

One plan provided for widows who lived in the United States and whose children were all under the age of fourteen. Under this plan, a widow with one child received $20 per month until the child turned fourteen, the age at which they were expected to find a job and earn income. The payment increased $5 per month for each additional child, up to four children. Families with five or more children received $40 per month. In most of these families, payments continued until the second eldest child turned fourteen.

The second type of payment was given as a lump sum. Childless widows and widows with children over the age of fourteen received a payment that varied in amount. If an immigrant widow decided to return to her birth country, she and her children were placed in the lump sum category.

Orphaned children also received a similar onetime payment, which was given to their legal guardian. No payment was made beyond the age of fifteen.

Despite the aid provided by the *Chicago Daily Tribune*'s relief fund, the Cherry Relief Commission, and other groups, without miners' wages, bereaved families still had no regular income. Almost three hundred families sued the St. Paul Coal Company for a monetary compensation in wrongful death lawsuits. The company offered to settle out of court for sums of up to $1,200, depending on the miner's marital status and the number of children he had. After mediation and negotiation, the company and most of the families agreed to a settlement based on the miners' yearly earnings. Some miners and families, however, further pressed their claim in court.

Most of the victims of the Cherry Mine disaster were immigrants from at least fifteen European countries. Only eleven of the victims had been born in America. Soon after the disaster, Cherry's mayor sent a letter to Scotland, to the father of Henry Stewart, one of the twelve rescue party members who burned to death in the hoisting cage. The mayor wrote, "We are giving every possible attention to Mrs. Stewart and the three children; and will see that they have every care. There is no praise great enough for Harry . . . who . . . risked [his life] repeatedly in bringing to the surface those few who were saved."

WHOSE FAULT?

On December 2, 1909, the coroner reopened his inquiry into the fire. For weeks, he and his jurors questioned miners, experts, company officials, and family members. They asked about the mine, what started the fire on November 13, and who was responsible. Two people who had firsthand knowledge never testified. Robert Deans and Alexander Rosenjack had fled Cherry believing that angry miners would kill them. Neither ever returned.

As part of its investigation into the fire, members of the coroner's jury went into the mine in April 1910. Even though they had heard testimony from many individuals, it was important for them to see the interior of the mine to resolve any questions regarding the mine's layout, condition, and equipment.

After many hours of testimony were recorded, several things were clear. Suffocation, burns, and cave-ins were the leading causes of death. Alex Norberg, John Bundy, Ike Lewis, and the nine men with them on and in the hoisting cage during the ill-fated rescue attempt died of burns. The confusing number of signal bells led to their deaths.

The coroner's jury found that a dripping torch set the bales of hay on fire. It further found that the burning car had been carelessly handled after the fire's discovery. Last, they declared that there was too long a delay between the fire's discovery and notifying the miners of the danger. Most of the victims could have escaped if a warning system had been in place. And routine fire drills, which were not practiced, would have made an orderly evacuation possible.

SAFE WORKING CONDITIONS

John Mitchell, a former president of the United Mine Workers of America, once said, "Coal mining is the most hazardous industry in America." From 1890 to 1909, 31,160 men were killed in coal mine accidents in the United States. In 1910, less than a year after the Cherry Mine fire, Mitchell reminded mine safety inspectors how important it was to prevent accidents:

> *The terrible mine catastrophe at Cherry suggests to our minds remedies for the prevention of similar occurrences. It is more valuable to society that the workers save their limbs and*

preserve their health. . . . To you men . . . belongs part of the task
of developing a uniform system of legislation for the protection
of miners . . . I urge you to do your part in making the United
States the safest and best protected nation in the world, instead
of the worst [regarding workplace safety].

Since then, members of the United Mine Workers of America have fought hard to improve working conditions and safety in US coal mines.

In March 1910, Illinois enacted a law that created the Mine Rescue Station Commission. This law—the first of its kind in the United States—required the construction of rescue stations where men learned how to respond to mine accidents.

Illinois miners lobbied for laws to protect them and to make their state's mines safer. By 1911, a number of new safety requirements for Illinois coal mines had become the law. Mines had to be inspected more frequently. Shafts had to be more accessible as escape routes, as did hoisting equipment. Clear signage and better stairways had to be installed. Extra ventilation had to be available and the bell signaling system altered to avoid confusion. Extra lighting and safety lamps were to be on hand. Mines had to have special refuge places where trapped miners could flee in case of an accident. All passageways had to be equipped with sprinklers, fire extinguishers, and telephones. Others states soon adopted these safety measures, which eventually became national laws.

Miners and their families also wanted to make sure that Cherry's disaster would set a precedent for the fair treatment of survivors and families of victims of future mining accidents. As a result, some companies in Illinois began the practice of providing a sum of money in the event of an employee's accidental death while at work. The compensation was often a certain times the amount of the employee's yearly wage. A. J. Earling, the president of the Chicago, Milwaukee, and St. Paul Railroad, acknowledged this as "a moral obligation" of his company with respect to Cherry Mine.

The Illinois state factory inspector discovered that the St. Paul Coal Company had hired boys under the age of sixteen. Ten underage boys were working in the mine at the time of the fire; four of them died. Since they had been illegally hired, the company was criminally liable. Families of these boys could seek compensation too. Families of the boys who died told the inspector the boys' true ages. Mary Buckel swore that John Bundy knew that her boys, Albert and Richard, were younger than sixteen when they were hired. The coal company admitted to violating the law. It was fined a total of $400 for the four boys who died; a fine totaling $600 was assessed in the cases of the six boys who escaped.

REMEMBER US

The Cherry Mine Disaster happened more than one hundred years ago. On November 13, 1911, thousands of people came to Cherry to dedicate a memorial statue to the memory of those who died in the mine. The statue stands at the edge of the Miners' Memorial Cemetery, just south of town. Lines of granite headstones, the names worn with age, mark the graves of some of the victims. Those in a language other than English remind us that many of our country's roots extend across oceans.

By July 1910, lines of gravestones filled Cherry's cemetery. Grave markers inscribed in languages other than English reflected Cherry's diverse community.

In 1911, a memorial stone was placed near the entrance to Miners' Memorial Cemetery in Cherry.

"TO THE MEMORY OF THE
MINERS WHO LOST THEIR
LIVES IN THE CHERRY
MINE DISASTER NOVEMBER
13, 1909."
"ERECTED BY THE U.M.W.
OF A. DISTRICT NO. 12,
ILLINOIS NOV. 13, 1911."

IN LATER YEARS

Albert Buckel did not return to the coal mine. He and his mother, Mary, moved to Peru, Illinois, some months after the fire. He worked as a laborer in a zinc factory and later as a tree trimmer. He died in 1927.

Robert Deans fled Cherry. For months, his whereabouts were a mystery. Later, it was reported that he had returned to Scotland. Scottish government records indicate that a man named Robert Deans, from Scotland, died during World War I.

George Eddy continued to work as a miner. He became trained and certified in mine rescue by the Mine Rescue Station Commission. He died in 1919.

Jessie Love remarried, as did many of the women widowed by the fire. She and her second husband, John Fraser, moved to southern Illinois. But mining still influenced her life: John was a mine boss, and her son, Morrison Love, was a miner too. Jessie died in 1947.

Giacomo Pigati, his brother Salvatore, and Antenore Quartaroli sued the St. Paul Coal Company. Fearing a court trial that would last months and cost a huge sum, the company agreed to a settlement with the three men that totaled $15,000. It was a record high for settlements against the company. Giacomo and his wife, Rosalie, had two children. He died in 1962 in Italy.

Salvatore Pigati left coal mining. Like the other survivors, he received compensation from the St. Paul Coal Company. He bought land in Illinois and became a farmer. Pigati married and had several children. He died in 1923.

Antenore Quartaroli and Erminia's second child, Geno, was born six months after Antenore's rescue. The couple later had a third son and a daughter, who was born during a family visit to Italy. Antenore Quartaroli continued to work as a coal miner. Eventually the family moved to Indiana. Antenore died in 1918 from complications following surgery. He was thirty-five years old.

Alexander Rosenjack went to Ohio, where his parents and other family members lived. He later moved to Michigan, where he worked as a streetcar motorman and mechanic. After his marriage in 1916, he moved to Battle Creek, Michigan, where he worked for thirty years for the city's fire department. Rosenjack died in 1957.

Walter Waite continued to work in the coal-mining industry. After he recovered from his entrapment, he served as a county inspector of mines. Following that, he was appointed state mine inspector, a job he held for more than a decade. He died in 1928.

Cherry Mine reopened in late 1910. The St. Paul Coal Company operated the mine and worked the third vein. The company closed the mine on April 30, 1927. A local man named John Bartoli bought the mine in 1929, operating it as the Cherry Coal Company. He ceased operation in 1934, and the mine closed completely in 1935. The tipple and other metal bits and pieces were sold for scrap iron. The shafts have been completely sealed and the mine buildings dismantled. Two large slag heaps remain as a reminder of the town's coal-mining days. To stabilize them and prevent landslides that could endanger Cherry residents, the piles have been planted with shrubs and trees and have become the home of many birds and wild creatures.

A SPECIAL AWARD

In 1910, thirteen men were awarded the Carnegie Medal for bravery during the Cherry Mine Disaster. This medal, given by the Carnegie Hero Fund Commission, acknowledges "civilians who risk their lives to an extraordinary degree saving or attempting to save the lives of others." All but two of the men who received the Carnegie Medal for their bravery at Cherry died in the mine. The honorees were:

John Bundy, mine manager

Robert Clark, miner

George Eddy, mine examiner and fire boss (survived)

John Flood, clothing and shoe store owner

Dominick Formento, grocery store owner

Isaac Lewis Jr., livery stable owner

Andrew McLuckie, miner

J. Alexander Norberg, assistant mine manager

James Speir, miner

Henry Stewart, miner

John Szabrinski, cager

Charles Waite, mine examiner

Walter Waite, assistant mine manager (survived)

AUTHOR'S NOTE AND ACKNOWLEDGMENTS

I live about fifty miles from Cherry, Illinois. In 2002, I read Karen Tintori's book *Trapped: The 1909 Cherry Mine Disaster*. The book interested me because my great-grandfather was a hoisting cage engineer in a coal mine in Pennsylvania. Family stories say his wife was thankful that his job kept him aboveground. Tintori's story quickly riveted my attention.

One afternoon not long after I finished reading the book, my husband and I drove to Cherry. Miles before we reached town, we saw the two enormous slag heaps. Like mountains, they jut above an area that is pancake-flat for miles.

Cherry is a small town now, with less than five hundred people living there. The brick school that Albert Buckel and Alfred Howard attended is closed; school-age children are bused elsewhere. Some houses built for miners remain, with new families filling them. But the row of identical houses on Steele Street, where the Loves lived, is gone.

A small museum dedicated to preserving the memory of the disaster has a number of artifacts and photos. It also houses a painstakingly accurate scale model of the mine and its buildings, built by Ray Tutaj Jr. Looking at the model enabled me to visualize and describe the buildings as I wrote this book.

In 2009, I attended the 100th Annual Cherry Memorial Day, sponsored by the United Mine Workers of America. During this event, hundreds of people visit Cherry to learn the story of the fire. While there, I sat next to a woman who graciously let me hold her grandfather's pocket watch. He died in the mine, and the watch had helped identify his remains. She said, "This is the first time this watch has been back to Cherry since it was removed from his body."

Several years ago when I was in England, some friends and I visited a coal mine. Before going into the mine, we had to remove all electronic devices—cameras, cell phones, watches. The danger of an electric spark accidently igniting a mine gas was taken very seriously. We descended in the hoisting cage to the bottom, almost three hundred feet beneath the surface. The air felt cool and slightly damp. It smelled earthy, like a large chunk of wet rock. The roadways felt closed in, and some of the rooms where miners had worked had low ceilings, so low I could not stand upright inside them. I saw the stable where the pit ponies lived. At one point, we turned off the miner's lamp on the front of our hard safety hats. I experienced firsthand the feeling of instant blindness that Antenore Quartaroli, Walter Waite, George Eddy, and the Pigatis knew. A dark room at night doesn't remotely compare. I was *very* glad to get back to the surface.

I visited Cherry several times so I could walk the streets, know how long it took the miners to walk to work, and better understand the mine's location relative to the town. In the Cherry Mine Disaster

Museum, DeAnn Pozzi showed me artifacts and shared her knowledge of the town and the fire. Her husband, Jim, met me at the gate to the old mine—it's private property now. He pointed out where the shafts and buildings had been and told me a number of stories about growing up in Cherry. Jim knew miner Peter Donna, who'd escaped with his father from the third vein at the disaster's start and later owned a junkyard. Jim and his friends got parts from Donna's yard and made a wheeled cart. They raced it down the slag heap slopes. (Their parents did *not* know.)

Jack Rooney, raised in Cherry, offered valuable insights into immigrant life in the town. His maternal grandparents emigrated from Italy and spoke Italian at home. Jack's mother didn't speak English until she started school. His grandfather was in the mine the day of the fire and got out. As a youngster, Jack lived next door to Peter Donna, who told him many stories about the mine. Thanks, Jack, for working with me to tentatively identify the mystery woman as Alice Mills!

The Bureau County Historical Society in Princeton, Illinois, has a great collection of mine disaster photos and articles. Thanks to curator David Gugerty for pulling out the society's copy of the *huge* map titled *Map of Surface, St. Paul Coal Company's Mine No 2.* Its extraordinary detail holds a wealth of information about Cherry and its mine: the types of houses, the wells, the mine surface buildings, and the underground extent of the second and third veins.

As always, I loved exploring the collections found in several Illinois libraries. A hoisting cage loaded with thanks to the many wonderful librarians who helped me dig through the treasures in their collections. I first dipped my toes into Cherry Mine materials at the Peru Public Library, where I found recorded interviews with some of Cherry's miners, including Peter Donna. It was fascinating to hear them describe their lives as coal miners and their experiences during the disaster. The Richard A. Mautino Memorial Library, in Spring Valley, has a large collection of photos and several mining artifacts. They also have a big chunk of coal! And you can't beat the collection of newspaper articles and family information at the Abraham Lincoln Presidential Library, in Springfield. The Edward Caldwell Cherry Mine Disaster Research Collection at the University of Illinois Library in Champaign holds a wealth of photo archives and documents.

Crucial to my research was being able to read the university's digital copy of the more than seven hundred pages of the coroner's inquest. The many testimonies in this document provided important information about the mine and people's actions before, during, and after the disaster. Testimonies by Jessie Love, Jemima Miller, Alice Mills, Janet Stewart, and Elizabeth Spier helped me develop the narrative for women's actions and their responses to the fire, as well as Robert Deans's behavior and flight from Cherry. All of the miners' and civilians' testimonies in this incredible document reflect the confusion and fear that reigned underground as the fire spread beyond control, as well as the concerns of the people aboveground who anxiously awaited news.

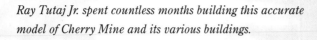

Ray Tutaj Jr. spent countless months building this accurate model of Cherry Mine and its various buildings.

SOURCE NOTES

Chapter 1: Saturday, November 13, 1909

p. 1: chilly air and a cloudy sky: *DeKalb (IL) Daily Chronicle*, November 13, 1909, 1.

p. 4: thirty-three identical houses: *Map of Surface, St. Paul Coal Company's Mine No. 2, Cherry, Bureau Co. ILL.*, collection at Bureau County Historical Society, Princeton, IL.

p. 5: Not far away . . . infant son: Quartaroli, 1.

p. 5: Some of the houses . . . were reassembled: Donna.

p. 8: In 1903, there was only a handful . . . country crossroads: "Smother Mine Fire at Cherry," *DeKalb (IL) Daily Chronicle*, November 15, 1909, 6.

p. 8: By the time Cherry was seven . . . to six hundred: No title, *Pratt (KS) Union*, November 2, 1905, 4.

Chapter 2: From Cornfields to Coal Mine

p. 11: "lean streaks . . . strip of bacon": Pierard.

p. 12: In 1860, US coal mines . . . wasn't enough: Curran, 23.

p. 14: year-round employment for up to seven hundred miners: "Money in a New Town," *Freeport (IL) Journal-Standard*, June 2, 1905, 2.

p. 21: diagram: Ross, 11.

p. 23: On December 11, 1905 . . . producing coal: Buck, 10.

p. 23: That year, miners . . . winner by 351 tons: "New Mine Breaks Hoisting Record," *Times* (Streator, IL), August 9, 1907, 4.

p. 23: "Within a few years Cherry . . . central west": "Money in a New Town," *Chicago Daily Tribune*, June 20, 1905, 5.

p. 29: "Never before in the history . . . of Europe": editorial, *Bureau County Tribune* (Princeton, IL), May 29, 1903, 4.

Chapter 3: Into the Mine

p. 33: After the slag was removed . . . $3.50 each: Donna.

p. 33: 1,500 tons of coal per day: Stratton, 5.

pp. 50: Thorne hitched his mules . . . snatched a bite: Charles Thorne testimony, *Inquest*, 26.0

Chapter 4: Trouble

pp. 54, 56: "Bring your pail . . . water," "We tried . . . sump for water," "You'd better [h]eave us up," "No, they may get . . . work again," and "I am going . . . come out": Alfred Buckel testimony, *Inquest*, 489–490.

p. 58: "[We have] a car . . . afire" and "Let it fall down": William Smith testimony, *Inquest*, 471.

p. 59: "Look out!": ibid.

p. 60: "the whole air course . . . afire" and "it was best . . . they could": Andrew Lettsome testimony, *Inquest*, 6.

p. 61: "I am getting . . . air-shaft stairs": Wyatt, 477.

p. 61: "I won't go . . . this mine": ibid., 478.

Chapter 5: Meanwhile, Confusion

p. 65: "What's the trouble here?" and "[There's a] car . . . below": Herbert Lewis testimony, *Inquest*, 664.

p. 65: "They are all lost down there": Martin Powers testimony, *Inquest*, 376.

p. 65: "Hoist the men, not the coal!": Wyatt, 476.

p. 66: Timbers in the air shaft caught fire . . . an inferno: Stratton, 6.

pp. 66–67: The fan's metal blades . . . crowd of people: Buck, 47.

p. 67: "The men are burning . . . do it quick!": ibid., 46.

p. 67: "Do you have a team [of horses] here?" "Yes," and "Go to my barn . . . down below": Herbert Lewis testimony, *Inquest*, 664.

p. 70: "Oh, they say there is . . . in it, too," "Oh, it couldn't . . . as that," and *Oh, God! . . . in the fire*: Wyatt, 483.

p. 71: "Could I be of any [help] down there?": Lyston D. Howe testimony, *Inquest*, 583.

p. 72: Suddenly, he kicked something . . . stimulate his circulation: Wyatt, 480.

p. 72: He wrapped a wet rag . . . hands and face: Buck, 60–61.

p. 73: "You go this way . . . entrance again": "Was Buried Seven Days in Coal Mine," *Chicago Daily Tribune*, December 4, 1909, 1.

p. 73: "Let me stay . . . do what I can": "Seek Survivors in Pit of Death," *Chicago Daily Tribune*, November 15, 1909, 2.

p. 73: "crowd of panic stricken miners": "Dread Gas Stops Cherry Rescues," *Chicago Daily Tribune*, November 21, 1909, 2.

p. 73: "Stand back from the flame!" and "My God . . . these fellows back": ibid.

p. 74: "nearer and nearer": Ross, 22.

p. 75: "They will need . . . down here": "Mine Tragedy at Cherry," *DeKalb (IL) Daily Chronicle*, November 15, 1909, 6.

p. 77: "Pound on the pipe . . . from below": Herbert Lewis testimony, *Inquest*, 666.

p. 77: "Come over . . . coming out": Lyston D. Howe testimony, *Inquest*, 588.

p. 77: "For God's sake . . . will die": Herbert Lewis testimony, *Inquest*, 667.

Chapter 6: Trapped!
pp. 81–82: "smoke in volumes" and "knew by . . . timber burning": John Barron, "It's Like This," *Daily News Tribune* (LaSalle, IL), November 12, 1975, 4.

p. 82: "It made our eyes . . . ran from them": Thomas White and Louis Murphy, "Eight Days in a Burning Mine," *Wide World Magazine*, October 1911, 586.

p. 82: John Lorimer grabbed the signal . . . rang three times: ibid.

p. 83: Salvatore held his coat sleeve over his mouth: Quartaroli, 3.

p. 83: "Stand back from the flame!": "Dread Gas Stops Cherry Rescues," *Chicago Daily Tribune*, November 21, 1909, 2.

p. 84: "We are caught . . . seeing the mules": Wyatt, 485.

p. 85: "hurried them . . . at top speed": "Mine on Fire Entombs 391," *Chicago Daily Tribune*, November 14, 1909, 2.

p. 86: Elizabeth had been napping . . . soon find him: "Rescue Party Finds Men Alive in Cherry Mine," *Streator (IL) Daily Free Press*, November 25, 1909, 1.

p. 87: "crushing the chest": Thomas White and Louis Murphy, "Eight Days in a Burning Mine," *Wide World Magazine*, October 1911, 589.

p. 87: "as if the earth were whirling": Quartaroli, 4.

p. 87: One man hadn't been too hungry . . . some tea: "Lack of Hunger Saves His Life," *Chicago Daily Tribune*, November 22, 1909, 2.

p. 88: "Alive at 10:30 yet . . .": All passages from Sam Howard's diary are from "Dying Miner's Diary Details His Fight for Life; Thinks of Fiancee to Last." *Chicago Daily Tribune*, November 24, 1909, 4, and "Third Level Silent Tomb," *Streator (IL) Daily Free Press*, November 24, 1909, 1.

Chapter 7: Black Damp

p. 91: Almost a mile . . . and a small notebook: Quartaroli, 5–6.

p. 91: "I know Maggie . . . Tom White": Thomas White to his wife, facsimile, Cherry Mine Disaster Museum, Cherry, IL.

p. 91: "We have poor . . . best of us": John Lorimer to his wife, facsimile, Cherry Mine Disaster Museum, Cherry, IL.

p. 92: "I have tried . . . as you can": George Eddy to his wife, facsimile, Cherry Mine Disaster Museum, Cherry, IL.

p. 95: Newspaper reporters asked questions . . . set up cameras: John E. Williams, "Causes of the Cherry Disaster as Seen through the Eyes of a Practical Miner," selected articles by John E. Williams, from 1906 to 1912, vol. 1 (clippings pasted into a bound journal), Abraham Lincoln Library, Springfield, IL.

p. 95: Gawkers began arriving . . . and dinners: Donna.

pp. 96–99: More than a dozen men volunteered . . . Monday morning, this time in the hoisting shaft: Buck, 80–83.

pp. 99–100: "I am hungry . . . Antenore": Antenore Quartaroli to his wife, facsimile, translated into English from the original Italian, Cherry Mine Disaster Museum, Cherry, IL.

p. 100: About 5:00 p.m. . . . just inside the chamber's entry: Quartaroli, 7–8.

Chapter 8: Cold, Hungry, Weak, Sick
p. 105: Earlier that same . . . *hunger*, he thought: Quartaroli, 9.

p. 105: "We all gave . . . man drank it anyway: "Find 22 Alive in Mine Tomb; More Signal?" *Chicago Daily Tribune*, November 21, 1909, 2, and "Was Buried Seven Days in Coal Mine," *Chicago Daily Tribune*, December 4, 1909, 1.

p. 107: One man later testified . . . his testimony. Rosenjack agreed: Martin Powers testimony, *Inquest*, 383.

p. 108: "Give me back . . . my husband": Buck, 96.

p. 110: Early Monday morning . . . grief and hopelessness": "Nurses in Heart of Sorrow," *Chicago Daily Tribune*, November 17, 1909, 2.

p. 111: Men rode horseback to the surrounding . . . cooked and ready to eat: "Officials Fear Riots at Cherry," *DeKalb (IL) Daily Chronicle*, November 16, 1909, 6.

pp. 112–113: By 7:00 Monday evening . . . many people already suspected: "Taking the Dead Out of Cherry Mine," *Bureau County Tribune* (Princeton, IL), November 19, 1909, 1 and 6.

p. 113: With the mine shafts sealed . . . pray to God for his life": "Entombed Miners' Letter of Farewell," *Chicago Daily Tribune*, November 22, 1909, 3.

p. 113: Earlier, a man . . . Robert didn't have any: Jessie Love testimony, *Inquest*, 516–520.

p. 114: "Dear Sister-in-law . . . Pigati": Salvatore Pigati to his sister-in-law, translated into English from the original Italian, Cherry Mine Disaster Museum, Cherry, IL.

Chapter 9: Eating Sunshine
p. 116: The men searched farther away . . . squeezed out every drop: "Rescuers Find 21 Men Alive in Mine," *McHenry (IL) Plaindealer*, November 25, 1909, 2.

p. 117: "This is the fourth day . . . bring us together": Giacomo Pigati to his wife, translated into English from the original Italian, Cherry Mine Disaster Museum, Cherry, IL.

p. 118: At 2:30 a.m. . . . 250 pine coffins: "Chicago Water to Mine Fire," *Chicago Daily Tribune*, November 16, 1909, 1.

p. 118: Tuesday morning . . . wet, and cold: "Water Is Poured into St. Paul Mine to Quench Flames," *Mattoon (IL) Journal-Gazette*, November 16, 1909, 1.

p. 120: 110°F to 115°F: Rice, 27.

p. 122: Officials worried . . . might riot: "Officials Fear Riots," *DeKalb (IL) Daily Chronicle*, November 15, 1909, 1.

p. 122: Maude McGinnis, one of Pearl . . . comforted Jessie and her children: "Nurses in Heart of Sorrow," *Chicago Daily Tribune*, November 17, 1909, 2.

Chapter 10: Are You Asleep?
p. 126: "One poor Italian . . . stay in America": "Plan Dash Today for Mine Victims," *Chicago Daily Tribune*, November 18, 1909, 3.

p. 126: "There is a great deal . . . rescue tomorrow": ibid.

p. 129: Every so often, he called . . . stop that!" his companions called: Wyatt, 487.

p. 129: Ruggeri Buonfiglio took . . . wine to drink": "Was Buried Seven Days in Coal Mine," *Chicago Daily Tribune*, December 4, 1909, 1.

p. 130: Quartaroli and two others . . . little water seeped in: Quartaroli, 10.

p. 130: From time to time . . . quickly resealed the hole: "Find 22 Alive in Mine Tomb; More Signal?" *Chicago Daily Tribune*, November 21, 1909, 1.

Chapter 11: A Peculiar Button
p. 136: On Thursday, Frank Moy, a Chinese . . . help from China": "Chinese Merchants Give Aid," *Chicago Daily Tribune*, November 20, 1909, 6.

p. 138: As he walked the streets . . . home that he passed: Menietti, 44.

pp. 138–139: While he waited for his turn . . . source of water for the group: Quartaroli, 12.

p. 139: "We are better off . . . they ever had, yet": Wyatt, 488.

p. 140: "I am sorry to tell you . . . there is water": Quartaroli, 14.

p. 140: "a fiery furnace": ibid., 15.

p. 142: Suddenly, Malinda gasped . . . remained with her for the night: "Find More Bodies of Mine Victims," *Chicago Daily Tribune*, November 20, 1909, 6.

pp. 143–144: "After a week's work . . . Sunday or Monday": ibid.

p. 144: "There is not the slightest . . . the search": "Taking the Dead Out of Cherry Mine," *Bureau County Tribune* (Princeton, IL), November 19, 1909, 1.

Chapter 12: Mad Cheering

p. 145: "It's time to get up . . . another attempt": Quartaroli, 15.

p. 146: "I don't expect . . . I prefer death": ibid.

p. 147: "I ask those of you . . . the last chance": ibid., 17.

p. 147: "I will stay here . . . where I now lay": "Was Buried Seven Days in Coal Mine," *Streator (IL) Daily Free Press*, December 4, 1909, 5.

p. 153: "Brothers[,] have courage . . . you good luck": Quartaroli, 17.

pp. 158–160: Following Clelland's directions . . . Dumont died shortly afterward: The quotations and description of the barricaded men's rescue are from "Priest Tells Rescue Story," *Chicago Daily Tribune*, November 21, 1909, 3, and Thomas White and Louis Murphy, "Eight Days in a Burning Mine," *Wide World Magazine*, October 1911, 594.

p. 161: "mad cheering . . . number was large": ibid.

p. 161: "I'm not going out . . . join a rescue party: "Priest Tells Rescue Story," *Chicago Daily Tribune*, November 21, 1909, 3.

pp. 161–162: "They have found . . . men are alive!" "hope gave wings to my feet," and "It was a relief . . . with lighter hearts": "Miss Eddy Tells Story," *Streator (IL) Free Press*, December 30, 1909, 2.

p. 162: turned back for another . . . wrapped in blankets": "Hymn Gives Hope to Entombed Men," *Chicago Daily Tribune*, November 21, 1909, 3.

pp. 162–163: "all those who were dear to my heart" and "It was a joy . . . together again": Quartaroli, 19.

p. 163: "It was 9 o'clock . . . visit my father": "Miss Eddy Tells Story," *Streator (IL) Free Press*, December 30, 1909, 2.

p. 165: Earlier that day, Jessie . . . told him to stay away: There is some confusion about when Jessie Love received the letter from her brother Robert Deans. In her testimony at the coroner's inquest, she said she received the letter on Saturday (November 20), two days after Deans left Cherry. On November 25, 1909, in an interview with a reporter from the *Chicago Daily Tribune*, on page 2 the reporter states she received the letter on November 23. I chose to use the date implied in Love's testimony, since it was given under sworn oath. Plus, the brother and sister's close relationship would seem to indicate that he wouldn't waste time in letting her know he was safe.

Chapter 13: More Flames

pp. 166–167: A Lithuanian miner . . . good night's sleep: "Pierce 3rd Vein; No Miners Alive," *Chicago Daily Tribune*, November 23, 1909, 2.

p. 167: Mine inspectors forbade . . . dangerously high: "Dread Gas Stops Cherry Rescues," *Chicago Daily Tribune*, November 22, 1909, 1.

p. 167: Avoiding black damp . . . finding survivors in the second vein: ibid.

p. 170: Five-year-old Ladon . . . among her friends: "Fund for Cherry Grows by Leaps," *Chicago Daily Tribune*, November 21, 1909, 3.

pp. 170–171: "I know they are alive . . . will save him" and "The men they brought up . . . come up dead": "Dread Gas Stops Cherry Rescues," *Chicago Daily Tribune*, November 22, 1909, 1 and 2.

p. 173: "I believe they are all dead . . . is now alive": "Waite Doubts If More Live," *Chicago Daily Tribune*, November 23, 1909, 2.

p. 176: "Sam and I were going . . . proud of him": "Dying Miner's Diary Details His Fight for Life; Thinks of Fiancee to Last," *Chicago Daily Tribune*, November 24, 1909, 4.

p. 178: 107°F: Rice, 40.

Chapter 14: Widows, Orphans, Blame

p. 184: "Any great disaster . . . American people": Bicknell, 7.

p. 186: "holding of families . . . home life": ibid., 12.

p. 187: "We are giving every possible . . . few who were saved": Stewart, 5.

p. 189: "Coal mining is the most . . . in America": Wyatt, 491.

p. 189: From 1890 to 1909 . . . in the United States: Clarence Hall and Walter O. Snelling, *Coal-Mine Accidents: Their Causes and Prevention*, Department of the Interior, United States Geological Survey, 1907, Bulletin no. 333, 5, and "Coal Fatalities for 1900 through 2019," United States Department of Labor, accessed online July 20, 2020, https://arlweb.msha.gov/stats/centurystats/coalstats.asp.

pp. 189–190: "The terrible mine . . . worst [regarding workplace safety]": "U.S. Lags in Laws, Mitchell Claims," *Chicago Daily Tribune*, June 16, 1910, 13.

p. 190: By 1911, a number . . . fire extinguishers, and telephones: Stratton, 7.

p. 191: "a moral obligation": J. E. William, "The Cherry Settlement," *The FRA* 4, no. 3 (1910): 93.

p. 191: Mary Buckel swore that . . . when they were hired: "Child Labor Laws Were Violated," *Evening Telegraph* (Dixon, IL), November 18, 1909, 3.

p. 191: It was fined a total . . . boys who escaped: "Coal Company Fined $400 for Boys' Deaths at Cherry," *Chicago Daily Tribune*, June 21, 1910, 3.

A Special Award

p. 197: "civilians who risk their lives . . . of others": Carnegie Hero Fund Commission, www.carnegiehero.org/.

BIBLIOGRAPHY

Ardeni, Pier Giorgio. *Across the Ocean to the Land of Mines: Five Thousand Stories of Italian Migration from the Mountains of Bologna and Modena to America at the Turn of the Twentieth Century.* Bologna, Italy: Edizioni Pendragon, 2015.

Bicknell, Ernest Percy. *The Story of Cherry: An Account of the Great Disaster of November 13, 1909, and the Measures of Relief and Rehabilitation Employed.* Washington, DC: American Red Cross, 1911.

Buck, Frank P. *The Cherry Mine Disaster.* Chicago: M. A. Donohue, 1910.

"The Cherry Mine Disaster." *Mines and Minerals.* December 1909, 296–297.

"The Cherry Mine Disaster." *Mines and Minerals.* February 1910, 423–428.

Curran, Daniel J. *Dead Laws for Dead Men: The Politics of Federal Coal Mine Health and Safety Legislation.* Pittsburgh: University of Pittsburgh Press, 1993.

Donna, Peter. *Cherry Mine Disaster and Coal Mining: An Oral History Interview.* Oral History Tape Number TC OH 6 DON, Tape Number 6, transcription of interview of May 1975. Starved Rock Library System History Collection, Ottawa, IL. Accessed at Peru Public Library, Peru, IL.

Inquest Proceedings Taken before Coroner A. H. Malm at Wiebold's Hall, Cherry, Illinois . . . December 2nd, 1909. Edward Caldwell Cherry Mine Disaster Research Collection, 1909–2007, University of Illinois at Urbana-Champaign.

Menietti, Celestino. *Cherry Mine Disaster and Coal Mining: An Oral History Interview.* Oral History Tape Number TC OH 43 MEN, transcription of interview of September 22, 1975. Starved Rock Library System History Collection, Ottawa, IL. Accessed at Peru Public Library, Peru, IL.

Peterson, Harry. "Case for Legacy of Massive Mine Fire Built by Grandson of Disaster's Hero." *imPULSE*, Newsletter of the Carnegie Hero Fund Commission, issue 37, March 2014, 11–14.

Pierard, Jule. "Operation of Cherry Mine, Cherry, Illinois: An Oral History Interview." Oral History Tape Number TC OH 15 PIE, Tape Number 15, transcription of interview of July 1975. Starved Rock Library System History Collection, Ottawa, IL. Accessed at Peru Public Library, Peru, IL.

Quartaroli, Antenore. *Diary. Great Disaster of the Cherry, Ill. Mine.* Translated by Mary Muzzarelli. Unpublished. Spiral-bound copy in Peru Public Library, Peru, IL.

Rice, George. *The Cherry Mine Disaster.* No publisher given, 1910. Edward Caldwell Cherry Mine Disaster Research Collection, 1903–2007. University of Illinois at Urbana-Champaign.

Ross, David, and State Board of Commissioners of Labor, Illinois Bureau of Labor Statistics. *Report on the Cherry Mine Disaster.* Springfield, IL: Illinois State Journal Co., State Printers, 1910.

Stewart, W. S. *Price of Coal Paid by the Love Family and Other Scottish Miners at Cherry Mine Disaster Illinois on 13th November 1909.* Sandbach, Cheshire, UK: W. S. Stewart, 2009.

Stratton, Christopher. *The Cherry Mine (St. Paul Coal Company No. 2), Cherry, Illinois.* Illinois Department of Natural Resources Cultural Resource Management Program Abandoned Mined Lands Reclamation Cultural Resources Evaluation. Prepared by Fever River Research. Springfield, IL: Illinois Department of Natural Resources, 2002.

Tintori, Karen. *Trapped: The 1909 Cherry Mine Disaster.* New York: Atria Books, 2002.

Turner, Janine. "Proving of a Hero." Unpublished manuscript in possession of the Cherry (IL) Public Library.

Tutaj, Ray, Jr. "St. Paul Coal Mine in Cherry, Illinois (Part 1)." *Model Railroading*, December 2000/ January 2001, 24–27.

———. "St. Paul Coal Mine in Cherry, Illinois (Part 2)." *Model Railroading*, January/February 2001, 24–31.

United States Census Records, 1880–1940.

Wyatt, Edith. "Heroes of the Cherry Mine." *McClure's*, April 1910, 473–492.

IMAGE CREDITS

pp. 2, 10, 71, 94, 97, 101, 112, 119, 121, 143, 150–151, 163, 179, 181, 188, and front cover (middle): Courtesy of the Edward Caldwell Collection ID (MS 515), Illinois History and Lincoln Collections, University of Illinois at Urbana-Champaign Library

pp. 3 and 202–203: Courtesy of Sally M. Walker and the Cherry Mine Disaster Museum

pp. 4, 24–25, 32, 120, 127, 128, 148, 156–157, 169, 171, 174–175, front cover (top), and back cover: Courtesy of the Bureau County Historical Society, Princeton, Illinois

pp. 5, 6, 7, 22, 44, 82, and 83: Courtesy of the Knights of Pythias and the Cherry Mine Disaster Museum

p. 9: Courtesy of the *Freeport (IL) Journal Standard*

pp. 12, 27, 28, 34, 38–39, 43, 46 top and bottom, 49, and 75: Courtesy of the Library of Congress

pp. 13, 16, 17, and 78–79: Courtesy of the Abraham Lincoln Presidential Library and Museum, Cities and Towns Vertical File

pp. 33 and 37: Courtesy of the United States Department of Labor, Mine Safety and Health Administration

p. 42: Courtesy of Sally M. Walker and the Bureau County Historical Society, Princeton, Illinois

pp. 68–69, 134–135, 137, 141, 144, 182–183, and front cover (bottom): Courtesy of the Richard A. Mautino Memorial Library, Spring Valley, Illinois

p. 96: Courtesy of the Chicago History Museum, *Chicago Sun-Times/Chicago Daily News* collection, DN-0055352

pp. 124–125: Courtesy of the Chicago History Museum, *Chicago Sun-Times/Chicago Daily News* collection, DN-0055366

p. 164: Courtesy of the Cherry Mine Disaster Museum

p. 177: Courtesy of the Chicago History Museum, *Chicago Sun-Times/Chicago Daily News* collection, DN-0055450

p. 185: Courtesy of the Chicago History Museum, *Chicago Sun-Times/Chicago Daily News* collection, DN-0055361

pp. 192 and 193: Courtesy of Sally M. Walker

Every effort has been made to trace sources of images; the publisher would be happy to correct any omissions in future printings.

IMAGE CREDITS

pp. 2, 10, 71, 94, 97, 101, 112, 119, 121, 143, 150–151, 163, 179, 181, 188, and front cover (middle): Courtesy of the Edward Caldwell Collection ID (MS 515), Illinois History and Lincoln Collections, University of Illinois at Urbana-Champaign Library

pp. 3 and 202–203: Courtesy of Sally M. Walker and the Cherry Mine Disaster Museum

pp. 4, 24–25, 32, 120, 127, 128, 148, 156–157, 169, 171, 174–175, front cover (top), and back cover: Courtesy of the Bureau County Historical Society, Princeton, Illinois

pp. 5, 6, 7, 22, 44, 82, and 83: Courtesy of the Knights of Pythias and the Cherry Mine Disaster Museum

p. 9: Courtesy of the *Freeport (IL) Journal Standard*

pp. 12, 27, 28, 34, 38–39, 43, 46 top and bottom, 49, and 75: Courtesy of the Library of Congress

pp. 13, 16, 17, and 78–79: Courtesy of the Abraham Lincoln Presidential Library and Museum, Cities and Towns Vertical File

pp. 33 and 37: Courtesy of the United States Department of Labor, Mine Safety and Health Administration

p. 42: Courtesy of Sally M. Walker and the Bureau County Historical Society, Princeton, Illinois

pp. 68–69, 134–135, 137, 141, 144, 182–183, and front cover (bottom): Courtesy of the Richard A. Mautino Memorial Library, Spring Valley, Illinois

p. 96: Courtesy of the Chicago History Museum, *Chicago Sun-Times/Chicago Daily News* collection, DN-0055352

pp. 124–125: Courtesy of the Chicago History Museum, *Chicago Sun-Times/Chicago Daily News* collection, DN-0055366

p. 164: Courtesy of the Cherry Mine Disaster Museum

p. 177: Courtesy of the Chicago History Museum, *Chicago Sun-Times/Chicago Daily News* collection, DN-0055354

p. 185: Courtesy of the Chicago History Museum, *Chicago Sun-Times/Chicago Daily News* collection, DN-0055361

pp. 192 and 193: Courtesy of Sally M. Walker

Every effort has been made to trace sources of images; the publisher would be happy to correct any omissions in future printings.

INDEX

Page numbers in italics indicate images or captions